The
FRENCH
Diet

⚜

The
FRENCH
Diet

*The Secrets of Why French
Women Don't Get Fat*

Michel Montignac

LONDON, NEW YORK, MUNICH,
MELBOURNE, DELHI

Senior Editors Barbara Berger, Jennifer Williams
Interior Design Sherry Williams and Tilman Reitzle / Oxygen Design
Recipe Consultants Wesley Martin, Barbara Bowman
Editorial Assistant John Searcy
DTP Designer Milos Orlovic
Jacket Design Jeremy Canceko
Production Manager Ivor Parker
Project Director Sharon Lucas
Art Director Dirk Kaufman
Creative Director Tina Vaughan
Publishing Director Carl Raymond

Published in the United States by DK Publishing, Inc.
375 Hudson Street, New York, New York 10014

ISBN 0-7394-6209-1

Printed in the USA

Contents

Introduction

FRENCH PEOPLE ARE CERTAINLY NO BETTER than anyone else, yet it can be argued that there is an area where their wisdom excels: food. No one loves to eat more than the French. French culture enshrines food, but at the same time the French manage (infuriatingly) to stay slim and healthy. How is this possible? French people eat a wide variety of foods, drink wine on a daily basis, and take the time to eat structured, cooked meals. Two-thirds of them even go back home to cook and eat their lunch every day. If the French are spending so much time eating great food and rarely exercising, you would expect them to be more prone to developing the metabolic diseases that other Western countries suffer from. Surprisingly, the result is exactly the opposite: The French have one of the lowest rates of obesity and diabetes in the world. And, thanks to the "French paradox," their cardiovascular risk factor is three times less than that of Americans.

What's the Secret?

French people are slim because they make good food choices. Instead of being obsessed with calorie counting, flogging themselves at the gym for hours, or, worse, avoiding the foods they love, the French simply eat the "right" carbohydrates and fats. And because good food is venerated in France, it is eaten with great pleasure—and without guilt or the horrible compulsion to deprive oneself of the foods one loves in order to look and feel slim. Eating delicious, healthy food in satisfying portions three times a day is the basis of a lifestyle that has made the French the envy of the world, much to the annoyance of almost everyone! This completely balanced approach to food was popularized in 1986 with the publication of *Dine Out And Lose Weight*—the only diet that results in weight loss for good.

I know it works—because I wrote the book and lost 35 pounds in three months. For the last 20 years, I've kept the weight off, too. The beauty of my method is its simplicity: You don't have to wrack your brain to learn complicated formulas or count calories. It's all about eating and enjoying the right food.

My family has a history of obesity. Growing up fat in France, where obesity is rare, I was perpetually teased by my classmates. At 15, I swore I would never become a fat adult and threw myself into a desperate quest for the perfect diet. Over the course of the next decade or more I went on dozens of diets and bought over 300 diet books. Despite my best efforts, I was still overweight at age 35. It didn't help that I ate out regularly while working and traveling for a large multinational pharmaceutical company. Luckily, I had access to the company's science library, where I pored over study after study to try to understand why I couldn't lose weight. I was particularly intrigued by the research connecting obesity to adult-onset diabetes (approximately 90% of adults with diabetes are obese). I put myself on the diet that diabetics follow in order to control blood-sugar levels, and began to eat more fresh fruit, vegetables, and whole grains. I also consulted a guide called the Glycemic Index (GI), which ranks carbohydrates from 0 to 110 on how much they raise blood sugar. For example, a baked potato ranks 95, and is therefore a "bad" carbohydrate. Whole-wheat pasta, on the other hand, is a "good" carbohydrate and ranks 45. I also incorporated low-fat and high-fiber foods into my diet, while avoiding the pitfalls of eating sugary desserts and other sweets. One thing I didn't do was restrict the amount of food I ate. I am convinced now—as I was then—that counting calories is not the way to lose weight. Just take a look at the numbers: In the last century, Americans have actually decreased their caloric intake by as much as 30%, and yet there are more obese people in the US than anywhere else in the world.

Dine Out And Lose Weight, which I wrote not only for myself but for other people who had gained too much weight from heavy business lunches, was so successful that I wrote a second book for a more general audience, *Eat Yourself Slim,* in 1987. The book was a bestseller in 40 countries. Since then I've published more than 20 books that have sold millions of copies around the world—further evidence, I believe, that traditional, low-calorie diets are not delivering on their promise.

How did we get into this mess?

We seem to live in contradictory times. While our life expectancy is continually rising, our health is deteriorating. This is due in part to genetic factors. In the past—seen from a Darwinian perspective—only the fittest living organisms produced physically robust offspring, thus ensuring the survival of their own species. Since medicine has made enormous progress in the last 60 years, most people in industrialized countries have a longer-than-ever life expectancy. Paradoxically, this has led to more susceptibility to disease because our immune systems have become weakened through overuse of antibiotics. At the same time, bacteria are developing more quickly, and are becoming more resistant.

The second reason for our poor health is the quality of the food we eat, which has deteriorated over the last 50 years. In order to produce enough food to meet our demands—as well as to make sure it survives the rigors of handling and shipping—commercial growers rely on sturdy vegetables, fruit, and grains that give good yields, but which don't necessarily deliver all the nutrients, vitamins, and minerals that are essential to good health.

The massive use of chemicals and chemical processes in agriculture has had undesirable effects on consumer health, too. Add to this mix problematic food-processing techniques such as heating, refining, hydrogenation, the use of additives to preserve food, gelling agents, and various taste enhancers, and the nutritional value of each food so-treated is clearly diminished. Eating fewer processed foods, particularly breads, crackers, chips, potatoes, soda, and sweets, for example, would make a huge dent not only in reducing obesity, but in improving our cardiovascular and general health as well.

We have known for a long time that diet is definitely a key to health. Diet can prevent illnesses, but it can also increase the risk of contracting them. In fact, the American Obesity Association has stated that the health ramifications of being obese are more serious than those associated with smoking and problem drinking. This message, however, has not been adequately conveyed to the public. One reason for this is that many doctors and dieticians spend very little time discussing preventive health care with their patients. Most are trained to practice in an orthodox way and treat the symptoms of illnesses rather than delving into their causes. In other words, their therapeutic approach is limited almost exclusively to prescribing medications. This attitude seems especially wrong-headed when you consider simple dietary recommendations that could be made to help combat "diabesity," a new term that has been coined to describe the common concurrence of diabetes and obesity—a condition that afflicts over nine million Americans. For example, research studies have made a convincing case for the health benefits of eating high-fiber foods, not the least of which are weight loss and long-term weight maintenance. It has been shown that eating high-fiber foods decreases blood-sugar levels and lowers blood pressure, while decreasing hunger and enhancing the sensation of feeling "full" between meals.

Why we keep getting fat

The real reason why so many people these days have metabolic disorders such as obesity and type 2 diabetes is because diet experts have been telling us for half a century that we eat too much—above all too much fat—and that we don't get enough exercise. If this is true, why has the incidence of obesity and diabetes increased four-fold during this period—even after reducing the number of calories we consume by one third? At least there has been some dissent in the ranks in the last ten years or more: In 1993, Professor Marion Apfelbaum, Director of the Department of Nutrition of the Bichat Hospital in Paris, admitted publicly that nutritionists "have been totally wrong" about focusing on calories. At the same time, we're eating more reduced-fat, low-fat, and artificially sweetened foods—and we're still getting fat…and feeling guiltier about it than ever. Ongoing accusations that lack of exercise and a sedentary lifestyle play an equal role in keeping us fat only serve to deepen our misery. What you don't hear about as often are the statistics showing that even some people whose professions keep them relatively active are getting fat. The answer is simply that a low-fat, high-carbohydrate diet is disastrous both for our health and our waistlines.

Despite caveats from nutrition experts whose research and studies have successfully demonstrated the dangers of this diet, new potentially dangerous ones have sprung up to take its place. Now, for example, the adherents of both no-carbohydrate and low-carbohydrate diets are taking the stage. What is particularly mystifying about the advent of these diets is the fact that we have known since 1981 that not all carbohydrates are evil: Some are simply healthier than others. But before you throw out your grill and embrace carbohydrates once again as the panacea for a lifetime of health and slimness, remember what has happened with fat. First it was considered healthy, in an unqualified way, by almost everybody. Then, about 25 years ago, cardiologists decided that all fat was bad. But once it became known that olive oil and fish fats actually help reduce the risk of heart and cardiovascular disease, they changed their minds. Today cardiologists recommend that some fats should be required in any diet. A similar distinction is now being made between "good" and "bad" carbohydrates.

Telling "good" from "bad" carbs

We have known for almost 20 years that carbohydrates should be evaluated according to how they increase blood sugar. The Glycemic Index (GI) is the standard for ranking carbohydrates based on their immediate effect on blood-sugar levels. Carbohydrates that break down easily during digestion have the highest GI—the blood glucose response is fast and high. Carbohydrates that break down less easily release glucose into the bloodstream in smaller amounts—thus avoiding sudden energy spikes—and have a low GI. These are the "good" carbs. In fact, for years epidemiologists have pointed out that carbohydrates with a low GI lead to a reduction in:

- hyperinsulinism (too high a level of insulin in the blood, a key factor in weight gain)
- type 2 diabetes
- high cholesterol and triglyceride levels
- high blood pressure

In addition, studies of epidemic illnesses show that there is a close connection between the number of cases and the extent of type 2 diabetes, obesity, and the risk of cardiovascular disease, and the consumption of high-GI carbohydrates. Given these findings, you'd think more research would be dedicated to exploring the entire spectrum of these amazing discoveries. Fortunately, the scene is rapidly changing, and the benefits of pairing low-GI carbohydrates with good fats, as I propose in *The French Diet,* is gaining ground.

The Promise

Given the epidemic of obesity in the United States, dramatic action needs to be taken. Thankfully, there are relatively straightforward means of fighting the dangerous food trends that have contributed so much to the increase in obesity, diabetes, and heart disease in the United States. It is time to discard antiquated ideas about diet and embrace a fresh approach. This is where the French Diet comes in: Once you begin eating normal portions of the right foods (low GI and good fat), not only will the sensation of eating be that much more pleasurable, but the health benefits will be life-changing. Happily, this can be achieved without depriving yourself of good food and without spending every waking hour at the gym. The first two chapters of *The French Diet* explain why traditional diets have failed, and explore the scientific evidence behind the phrase "you are what you eat." Chapters 3 and 4 provide the foundation for a new understanding of exactly how what we eat impacts our weight and health. These chapters explain the benefits of identifying and eating low GI foods and the right kinds of fats in healthy quantities and combinations. Complicated scientific details are distilled and simplified to make it easy to understand how your body actually works and what you can do to safely maximize weight loss and keep it off permanently.

Phase 1 of the French Diet (Chapter 5) is the weight-reduction portion of my program. In it, I explain how calories are not the deciding factor in weight gain—on the contrary, our excess weight is the result of eating foods that trigger metabolic mechanisms that cause our bodies to store fat. Phase 1 aims to change your eating habits by focusing on foods that help rebalance your metabolism. And because this is the French Diet, my method is based on eating delicious foods that you will want to continue eating long after you have met your weight-loss goals. The fundamental principle of Phase 1 is simple: The overall GI of a meal should be kept as low as possible without reducing normal carbohydrate intake. This can be achieved by taking care to select only carbohydrates with a low GI. Applying Phase 1 is not difficult: I'll give you lots of appetizing options for breakfast (which you should never skip), lunch (the biggest meal of the day) and dinner (lighter than lunch, but completely satisfying). I'll even give you some ideas about fast food à la French Diet, and how to handle social eating.

Phase 2 (Chapter 6) is where we work on stabilizing your weight. This is the fun part because the emphasis is on expanding the repertoire of foods you can now enjoy and still maintain your slim and healthy shape. Phase 2 allows you to widen your choice of carbohydrates and even enjoy a couple of glasses of wine with dinner without running the risk of destabilizing your newly established weight. However, this phase needs to be handled with care because, as you expand your options, it's all too easy to go overboard. For example, you'll need to exercise the same caution with foods containing white flour and sugar, as in Phase 1, but now that eating differently and healthily has become a reflex, you can guiltlessly indulge in the occasional rich dessert knowing that it's a pleasurable exception and that you have not compromised your diet. After all, the French Diet has nothing to do with deprivation and everything to do with creating a balance between enjoying delicious, healthy food and being actively engaged in life.

The menus and recipes in this book (Chapter 7), which include cocktail snacks and dips and chocolate desserts—are not the gastronomic equivalent of a hair shirt! Food should be enjoyed above all, and part of my mission in the French Diet is to impart the exquisite pleasures of preparing and savoring truly memorable meals while you lose weight. You will be surprised by the versatility of the recipes and menus, whether cooking for yourself, or for family and friends.

Without a doubt, the dietary principles and recipes in *The French Diet* will help you lose weight, keep the weight off, and develop healthy eating habits that can protect you from illness and disease, whatever your age. Along the way, my hope is that your appreciation for good food will lead to other sound and enjoyable lifestyle choices that will permanently impact the overall quality of your health. With so many benefits to be gained from such an exciting new way of eating and losing weight, where is the risk in giving it a try?

1

The American Paradox

ARLY IN 2002, PRESIDENT GEORGE W. BUSH began a health initiative called the Fitness Challenge, in response to the epidemic problem of obesity in America, especially among young people. According to the World Health Organization (WHO), the US has the highest rate of obesity in the world, increasing three-fold since the 1980s. Today, two-thirds of the US populace is overweight, and half of these are obese. Indeed, obesity has risen at an epidemic rate during the past 20 years, making it a national objective to reduce obesity among adults to less than 15% by the year 2010. But researchers indicate that the situation is worsening rather than improving. Predictions are alarming, with some studies forecasting that almost 100% of Americans will be obese by the year 2030 if the current trend goes unchecked. In fact, a recent *New York Times* article stated that for the first time in two centuries the current generation of children in America may have shorter life expectancies than their parents, according to a new report (lead by Dr. S. Jay Olshansky of the University of Illinois), which contends that the rapid rise in childhood obesity "could shorten life spans by as much as five years."

For the longest time, being overweight was seen purely as an aesthetic problem or as a disadvantage in daily life. The obese had difficulties walking, finding clothes that fit, and using public transportation. But now it's official: Obesity is a huge health-risk factor and, therefore, a very real cause for medical concern—especially when almost half a million deaths a year can be directly or indirectly linked to obesity. According to the Centers for Disease Control and Prevention (CDC) in Atlanta, this alarming figure represents a 33% increase since the beginning of the 1990s. It also amounts to over 8% of total health spending, compelling Americans to spend about $100 billion dollars a year on doctors, hospital stays, and work-related accidents. Given these appalling figures, it is a wonder that more has not been done to address the obesity crisis, especially in view of the recent campaign to reign in the tobacco industry and put the breaks on smoking— which claims approximately 440,000 lives every year, according to the CDC. In 2004, the number of deaths attributed to obesity—300,000 or more, depending on the source—are coming dangerously close to those ascribed to smoking as the leading cause of preventable death.

The point of bringing up all these scary numbers and statistics isn't to frighten you into losing weight! If anything, they're here to provide a context for the eating program I propose in *The French Diet*, which, by the way, isn't a "diet" to my way of thinking. It's more about making satisfying lifestyle choices instead of focusing on depressing food restrictions. The endgame is achieving better health and developing a more positive attitude about how you look and feel. I think that's what most people want. By the same token, it's important to understand why we feel the way we do about food, and why we've chosen to eat some foods and not others, especially when we're trying to lose weight.

The Root of the Problem

So where do modern ideas about food and weight gain come from, and when did the problem with food begin to kick in? Not surprisingly, the shift to industrialization and motorization that peaked early in the 20th century had a huge impact. With automation and faster forms of transportation at our disposal it became less necessary for our bodies to expend valuable calories on labor or travel. But the time and energy-saving innovations that made life so much easier didn't keep people from eating just as much as they always had, and, sadly, all those extra, unused calories got stored as fat. The proliferation of a raft of other labor- and energy-saving conveniences in the decades that followed—everything from elevators to centralized living and shopping, not to mention the advent of convenience foods and faster ways of preparing them—didn't help anyone get any slimmer or improve their health, either.

Inevitably the unsettling mathematical logic—*excess energy in the form of calories = fat*—became all too clear to scientists and researchers, and various weight-loss diets came into being as a result. The most influential of these was a reduced-fat diet developed by the American Heart Association (AHA), based on the research of Dr. Ancel Keys. In a now-famous study, conducted in the 1970s, Keys compared the rate of cardiovascular deaths in seven countries around the world and discovered that people who consumed fewer saturated fats and whole-milk products, and who ate more vegetables, fresh fruit, and nuts, seemed to have lower cardiovascular death rates. This was especially true of Mediterranean countries. In any case, these findings were institutionalized by the AHA, whose subsequent dietary recommendations influenced millions of Americans to follow low-fat, high carbohydrate diets.

What was the result? In the years since the Keys study, Americans have dramatically reduced their daily fat intake at home, in restaurants, at spas—where, incredibly, clients pay enormous sums of money in order to eat nothing—and through myriad weight-loss programs. And Americans are still battling their waistlines. The irony is that there are even more gyms in the US than there are diet centers. Roads, sidewalks, and parks are thronged with joggers, runners, power-walkers, cyclists, and roller-skaters, but even these near-obsessive activities are hardly making a dent in the big picture of American fitness and health. What's gone wrong?

Deconstructing the American Paradox

"Divergent Trends in Obesity and Fat Intake Patterns," a study conducted by Dr. Adrian F. Heini and Dr. Roland L. Weinsier and published in 1997 by *The American Journal of Medicine*, showed that between the late 1970s— when Ancel Key's work began influencing the way we eat—and the early 1990s, Americans reduced their fat consumption by 11%, and increased their consumption of calorie-reduced products from 19% to a whopping 76%! In the same period the number of obese people climbed by 31%.

The authors of the study were so surprised by these results that they called the study "The American Paradox." However, the American study merely confirmed what was already apparent in the US: Calorie intake had dramatically decreased while obesity was booming. At around the same time, a number of related studies showed that there is no correlation between weight gain and food intake. But what none of the studies could predict was the American food industry's reaction to this incredible data and the negative impact it would have on our health.

In a bid to steer Americans away from the dangers of high-fat foods, such as red meat, and to promote new eating trends that would reflect the low-fat, high-carbohydrate diet of countries like Japan—which have relatively low rates of obesity and cardiovascular disease—food manufacturers flooded the market with low-fat, highly processed foods. The problem with these tasty products, despite their accurate claims of being fat-free and low-cholesterol, was that they lacked the nutrients and fiber that made the Japanese diet healthier. In the US, manufacturers effectively stripped away the nutritional value of many foods through over-processing, and instead supplied consumers with a copious supply of "empty" calories. As a result, an enormous and immensely lucrative low-fat food industry was spawned, so that people could eat fat-free everything, from cookies and ice cream to brownies, crackers, and cakes—while believing this was healthy. What everyone forgot to think about was the number of calories, and the subsequent pounds, that these "fat-free" carbohydrates were delivering.

Pyramid power

Everyone has seen the little black triangles on the back of countless cereal boxes and food labels at the supermarket—the triangle is a familiar icon of daily life, especially if you do a lot of food shopping. Americans have been living by the "Food Guide Pyramid" since its conception in the 1960s by the US Department of Agriculture (USDA)—and yet for most people, the history of how and why it came into being is a little foggy.

From my point of view, the most interesting fact about the Food Guide Pyramid is that it came into being in order to address a dramatic increase in heart disease. A decade later, the USDA's deepening concern for this chronic illness was reflected in their recommendations to reduce the amount of fats, sweets, and alcohol that Americans consume. Still working from the premise that fats are the enemy, the Pyramid focused on fat because, as the guidelines state, "most Americans' diets are too high in fat" and "a diet low in fat will reduce your chances of getting certain diseases and help you maintain a healthy weight." Now here's the interesting part: "complex carbohydrates"—bread, cereal, rice, and pasta—form the all-important base of the Pyramid, representing the foods that Americans should eat in greater abundance than any other group (up to 11 servings a day).

We have seen all too clearly where
an emphasis on carbohydrates leads,
especially the refined variety: a spike in
blood-sugar levels that stimulates hunger
and encourages overeating and obesity.

Of course, the USDA did not set out to undermine the health of Americans. Their recommendations were undoubtedly made in good faith, but they were based on old dietary guidelines and questionable scientific evidence. Although the USDA is currently revising the pyramid, their guidelines have achieved the opposite effect of what they set out to do: Americans are fatter and less healthy than ever.

Rebuilding the Pyramid

Luckily, Americans have a powerful advocate in Dr. Walter C. Willett, Chairman of the Department of Nutrition and Professor of Epidemiology in the School of Public Health at Harvard University. Dr. Willett's observations, gleaned from tracking the diets and health of thousands of people for more than 20 years in the world-famous "Nurses' Health," "Physicians' Health," and "Health Professions Follow-up" studies, led him to become one of the most outspoken critics of the USDA food pyramid. In 2001, he and his colleagues created a rival pyramid called the Harvard School of Public Health Healthy Eating Pyramid, telling *USA Today:* "The USDA pyramid offers wishy-washy, scientifically unfounded advice on an absolutely vital topic—what we eat. At worst, the misinformation it offers contributes to obesity, poor health and unnecessary early deaths."

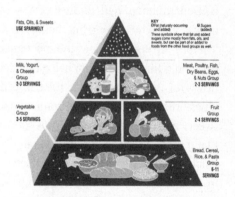

USDA Food Guide Pyramid
Source: U.S. Dept. of Agriculture/U.S. Dept. of Health and Human Services

Based on the best available scientific evidence about the links between diet and health, the new pyramid addresses fundamental flaws in the USDA pyramid and offers sound information to help people make better choices about what to eat. Willett and his colleague Marjorie McCullough looked at heart disease and cancer among people whose diets matched the USDA's recommendations and compared them to others who followed a Harvard-designed diet containing fewer carbohydrates and trans fats. The study found that those who followed the Harvard diet had a significantly reduced risk for major chronic disease. The Healthy Eating Pyramid turns the old USDA model on its head and shuffles around the kinds of foods that ensure good general health and a healthy weight. It prioritizes whole-grain food and plant oils; vegetables and fruits; nuts and legumes; fish, poultry, and eggs; and dairy or a calcium supplement; while the small top of the pyramid contains foods that should be eaten sparingly: red meat, butter, white rice, white bread, potatoes and pasta, and sweets.

GOOD CARBS AND HEALTHY FATS COME INTO THEIR OWN

The beauty of the Harvard pyramid is that it acknowledges how much the body needs carbohydrates for energy! The best carbs are found in whole grains (such as oatmeal, whole-wheat bread, and brown rice), because they keep blood sugar and insulin from rising to critical levels. Of course, better control of blood sugar and insulin can keep hunger at bay and help prevent the development of type 2 diabetes—all of which confirms the effectiveness of the French Diet, with its emphasis on low-GI carbohydrates and "good" fats that contain no trans-fatty acids. Harvard's revolutionary pyramid suggests that if you eat red meat every day, switching to fish or chicken several times a week can improve cholesterol levels. So can switching from butter to olive oil. I couldn't agree more: Take a look at my menus and recipes and tie on your apron. The Harvard pyramid even recommends alcohol in moderation, and this cheers me to the core, for there is nothing better than a wonderful glass of wine to accompany a healthy and delicious dinner à la French Diet. Bon appétit!

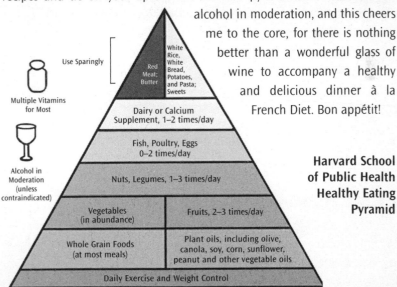

Harvard School
of Public Health
Healthy Eating
Pyramid

2
How Carbs Work: It's Quality, Not Quantity

PREVIOUSLY, IT WAS ASSUMED that all the calories counted on your plate had the same value, no matter what the food, and were automatically available to your body after consumption. Thanks to new knowledge about the digestive properties of foods, we now know that it isn't the calories or the quantity of food you eat but the quality—its nutritional content and value—that is important. This determines the way it is digested.

You Are What You Eat

Carbohydrate foods, which include sugars, starches, and fibers, are not inert substances—each bite you eat creates a metabolic reaction in your body. (In addition, the way and the extent a food is prepared, cooked, stored, and even cooled all impact its nutritional value, as we will see later.) Sugars and starches are processed differently by your digestive system, and some of them are more fat-inducing than others. In order to help you understand these reactions, it is first necessary to understand what is in the carbs you eat, so here is a brief, simple rundown:

SUGARS

Carbohydrates are made up of sugar molecules. Single sugars, also known as "simple" sugars, because they are composed of one sugar molecule, are called monosaccharides. The key monosaccharides in our diet are:

- glucose (found in most carbohydrate foods)
- fructose (found in fruits, vegetables, and honey)
- galactose (found in dairy products)

Sugars consisting of two molecules joined together are called disaccharides. The most common disaccharides are:

Sucrose (glucose + fructose)
WHERE IT IS FOUND: derived from sugarcane or beets, it also occurs naturally in most fruits and vegetables and is the main component in table sugar.

Lactose (glucose + galactose)
WHERE IT IS FOUND: dairy products

Maltose (glucose + glucose)
WHERE IT IS FOUND: beer and cereal (does not occur in nature but is formed by the enzymatic processing of starch)

STARCHES, FIBERS, AND GLYCOGEN

Then there are polysaccharides, which are chains of multiple sugar molecules, also called "complex" sugars or carbohydrates. The key ones in our diet are starch, cellulose, and glycogen.

Starch
Starch is the main polysaccharide that plants use to store glucose. When we eat starch, an enzyme called amylase found in our saliva and intestines breaks the starch down into glucose, which is then absorbed into the bloodstream. "Resistant" starches, such as those in legumes and unprocessed grains, are healthier and less fattening since they pass through the intestines with minimal digestion—and minimal impact on your blood-sugar level.
WHERE IT IS FOUND: grains, legumes, and vegetables

Fiber
Plants also contain the polysaccharide known as cellulose, which makes up the fibers that form plant cell walls and tissue. We cannot digest fiber—it passes through the digestive tract without being absorbed—but it is important because it helps keep the body from absorbing fat and cholesterol from food, as well as reducing heart disease, high cholesterol, and high blood pressure.
WHERE IT IS FOUND: fruits, vegetables, seeds, and nuts

Glycogen
Glycogen is the polysaccharide used by humans and animals to store energy. Excess glucose from consumed foods is bonded together to form glycogen molecules, which are stored in the liver and muscle tissue as an "instant" source of energy.
WHERE IT IS FOUND: in your body's liver and muscle tissue

Mashed Potatoes Vs. Lentils

Depending on its nutritional content, each food is processed differently by your body. After the enzymes, acids, and muscles in your stomach start to break down your food, it passes to the small intestine. Once in the intestine, other enzymes complete the process and the nutrients—sugars, fatty acids, and proteins, as well as trace vitamins and minerals—are absorbed into the bloodstream. Two foods in the same category (such as starch-rich carbohydrates), with the same number of calories, can vary overwhelmingly in the amount of glucose they release after digestion. As we will see, knowing the difference is key to understanding weight gain.

For example, on one plate we dish out a portion of plain mashed potatoes containing 264 calories as carbohydrates, and on another plate a portion of lentils, also containing 264 calories as carbohydrates. In the past, both portions would be considered interchangeable: both are starches, both are complex carbohydrates, and both contain the same number of calories. Why would one food be more fattening, ultimately, than the other, all things being "equal"?

Here's why: The amount of glucose that goes into your bloodstream during the digestion of lentils is *three times less* than when mashed potatoes are digested, making the actual calorie energy that is available for use by your body three times as high in potatoes as it is in lentils.

Carb/Calorie Counts for Mashed Potatoes and Lentils

	Mashed potatoes	Lentils
Total portion in grams to give the same amount of pure carbohydrate	200g	400g
Amount of pure carbohydrate (starch)	66g	66g
Calorie content of the carbohydrates on the plate	264 calories	264 calories
Number of calories available after digestion	250 calories	79 calories

INSULIN AND FAT STORAGE

Glucose is one of the body's main fuels and the brain's sole nutrient. It's also stored as glycogen in the liver and muscles for use as energy. In order to meet the body's requirements, the pancreas produces a hormone called glucagon, which keeps the amount of glucose in the bloodstream at a constant level of 70 milligrams per deciliter (mg/dL) to 110 mg/dL. This is called the glycemia or blood-sugar level. Each time you eat carbs, the glucose absorbed into your bloodstream after digestion causes a rise in the blood-sugar level. But this is a temporary state. After about 30 minutes, when the glucose has been absorbed completely, there's a glycemic (blood-sugar) peak. At that moment, the pancreas, one of our most important metabolic organs, secretes the hormone insulin.

Insulin's job is to lower glucose levels in the blood, bringing them back to the standard level—in a healthy body, the amount of insulin produced by the pancreas is precisely matched to the blood-sugar level. However, if the amount of glucose is too high, the insulin response will be huge and may trigger a mechanism that causes excess glucose to be turned into fat (a process called lipogenesis) that is itself stored in case of future need.

Now we can understand why eating two identical carbohydrates can lead to two different metabolic reactions:

- A portion of mashed potatoes leads to excess sugar (hyperglycemia) in the blood. This in turn leads to a high secretion of insulin, which can result in the excess sugar being stored as a fat deposit…leading to weight gain. The likelihood of weight gain is increased when carbs are eaten at the same time as fat, as in the case of deep-fried potatoes. Because of the presence of insulin, the fatty acids are stored rather than burned.

- A portion of lentils only slightly increases the blood-sugar level, leading to a low secretion of insulin.

Excess insulin causes weight gain. Years of eating too many carbs that induce a high glycemia can stress the body, causing the pancreas to produce more insulin than needed. This overproduction of insulin is called hyperinsulinemia. The residual insulin directs the excess energy of the digested food (carbs as well as fat) towards storage rather than burning. In addition to weight gain, hyperinsulinemia raises cholesterol levels and thickens arteries. It also causes sodium retention, raising blood pressure.

3

The Truth About Carbs

CARBOHYDRATES HAVE LONG BEEN DIVIDED into simple carbohydrates and complex carbohydrates because it was thought that foods with complex carbohydrate molecules, like potatoes, took longer to digest and therefore released sugars more slowly into your digestive system (and, supposedly, were not as liable to make you gain weight); and simple carbohydrates, like sugar, were digested more quickly. We now know that this is not the case—both are digested at the same speed.

In the previous chapter, we learned that the energy factor of a food—its calorie content—is not the deciding factor in weight gain, as has long been believed. It is the nutritional content that is important, because it determines the type of metabolic reaction a food causes. This reaction leads, in turn, to weight loss or gain. To help you lose weight the French way—and stay thin—you need to learn how to choose foods according to their metabolic potential.

THE MOST COMMON CARBS IN OUR DIET

Grains and cereals	wheat, rye, oats, but also corn and rice (flour, bread, and baked goods)
Tubers	potatoes, yams, Jerusalem artichokes
Root vegetables	carrots, white turnips, parsnips, rutabagas
Seeds and beans	dried beans, lentils, peas, chickpeas, soy beans
Fruit	apples, apricots, avocados, bananas, berries, figs, grapefruit, melon, peaches, pears, plums, nectarines, oranges
Vegetables	artichokes, asparagus, broccoli, cabbage, eggplant, green beans, peppers, tomatoes, zucchini, and all types of lettuce

The Glycemic Index (GI)

All food consists of macronutrients—carbohydrates, proteins, and fats—and micronutrients such as vitamins, minerals, and trace elements. The percentage differs depending on the food.

Since it is the carbohydrate content in food that primarily influences blood-sugar levels (called "glycemia"), the majority of carbohydrate foods can be measured according to how they influence blood-sugar levels. Using this criterion, carbohydrates have been arranged on a scale, referred to as the glycemic index (GI), which classifies carbohydrates according to their capacity to increase blood-sugar level. Each carbohydrate is ranked by comparing its effect on blood sugar to the effect of pure glucose, which has been arbitrarily assigned a ranking of 100. By choosing carbohydrates according to their GI, you can better control your blood-sugar levels as well as your weight.

If the GI of a food is very high, as is the case with French fries, whose GI value is 95, this means that the digestion of this carbohydrate will cause a big rise in blood-sugar levels, and therefore the body reacts by secreting a lot of insulin to help lower the high blood sugar. If the GI of a food is low, as is the case with lentils, whose GI value is 25, then digestion of this carbohydrate will release far less glucose and less insulin will be needed to break down the blood-sugar levels.

You can check the ranking of foods on the Glycemic Index Table, which you can find on the next four pages. Only carbohydrates or foods containing carbohydrates are evaluated according to the GI. In this list, therefore, you will only find foods that contain carbohydrates. Information on protein and fat can be found on pages 39–42.

NOTE: *Items that are starred: Although these items have a high GI, their pure carbohydrate content is very small. Consequently, eating a normal serving may have an insignificant impact on glycemia and insulin secretion.

GLYCEMIC INDEX (GI) VALUES TABLES

Carbohydrates with a High Glycemic Index	Glycemic Index
Corn syrup	110
Maltose (beer)	110
Glucose (dextrose)	100
Modified starch	100
Rice syrup	100
Cornstarch	95
Potato starch	95
Potatoes (scalloped, hash browns, and French fries)	95
Rice flour	95
Bread, gluten-free white	90
Potatoes, baked with skin	90
Rice pasta	90
Rice, sticky	90
Bread, hamburger buns, white-flour	85
Carrots, cooked	85
Cornflakes	85
Honey	85
Popcorn, without sugar	85
Pretzels	85
Puffed rice	85
Rice, instant	85
Rice pudding, made with short-grain rice	85
Wheat flour, bleached (in processed baked goods)	85
Turnips*	85
Tapioca	85
Crackers made from white flour	80
Lima beans, cooked	80
Lychees, canned	80
Potatoes, mashed	80
Puffed corn (breakfast cereal with sugar added)	80
Puffed wheat (breakfast cereal with sugar added)	80
Pretzels	80
Wonder Bread®	80
Pumpkin*	75
Sports drinks	75
Watermelon*	75
Waffles	75
Water crackers	75
Bagel	70
Baguette	70
Chocolate bar, milk chocolate	70

Croissant	70
Gnocchi	70
Millet	70
Noodles, pasta, white flour	70
Potato chips	70
Rice, instant	70
Risotto	70
Rutabaga	70
Shredded wheat	70
Soda (sugared)	70
Special K®	70
Sugar (sucrose)	70
Beets	65
Bread, whole-grain	65
Corn, on or off the cob	65
Couscous, cooked for five minutes	65
Jam, regular with sugar	65
Maple syrup	65
Muesli, regular	65
Potatoes, boiled in skins	65
Raisins, dark and golden	65
Ravioli, durum wheat	65
Rye crisp-bread	65
Sorbet, with sugar	65
Tortilla chips	65
Apricots, canned	60
Bananas, ripe	60
Barley flakes	60
Fruit cocktail, canned in sugar syrup	60
Ice cream, regular, with sugar	60
Melons (cantaloupe, honeydew)*	60
Oatmeal, from rolled oats	60
Orange juice, commercial, with sugar	60
Rice, long-grain	60
Semolina, white, cooked	60
Bulgur, cooked	55
Butter cookies	55
Papaya, fresh	55
Peaches, canned	55
Pears, canned	55
Shortbread	55
Spaghetti, non-whole-wheat, cooked well	55

Carbohydrates with a Low Glycemic Index

	Glycemic Index
All-Bran®	50
Apple juice	50
Barley, whole-grain	50
Brown rice, cooked	50
Kiwi	50
Mango, fresh	50
Pineapple juice, unsweetened	50
Sweet potatoes	50
Grapefruit juice, unsweetened	45
Grapes, green	45
Grapes, red	45
Orange juice, fresh-squeezed	45
Rye bread, whole-grain	45
Pineapple, fresh fruit	45
Rye, whole-grain	45
Apricots, dried	40
Bread, organic stone-ground sourdough	40
Buckwheat flour	40
Buckwheat pancakes	40
Buckwheat pasta	40
Carrot juice, fresh-pressed	40
Pinto beans, in salt water, canned	40
Kidney beans, canned	40
Lentils, green, in salt water, canned	40
Oat flakes, uncooked	40
Plum, dried	40
Pumpernickel bread	40
Sorbet, sugar-free	40
Spaghetti, durum wheat, cooked 5 minutes	40
Spaghetti, whole-wheat, cooked al dente	40

Carbohydrates with a Very Low Glycemic Index

	Glycemic Index
Apples, dried	35
Beans, pinto, dried, cooked	35
Beans (red, white, or black), cooked	35
Figs	35
Peas, fresh green	35
Oranges	35
Peas, dried, cooked	35
Plums	35
Quinoa, cooked	35
Tomato juice, unsweetened	35

Wild rice	35
Yogurt, whole milk and low-fat milk	35
Apples	30
Apricots, fresh	30
Beans, French (haricots verts), cooked	30
Beans, white, cooked	30
Carrots, raw	30
Chickpeas, cooked	30
Fruit spread without extra sugar	30
Garlic	30
Grapefruit	30
Lentils (brown, red, or yellow), cooked	30
Milk, skim	30
Mung beans, soaked, cooked for 20 minutes	30
Noodles, cellophane	30
Peaches	30
Pear	30
Peas, split, yellow, cooked for 20 minutes	30
Tomatoes	30
Cherries	25
Chocolate, dark (more than 70% cacao content)	25
Lentils, green, cooked	25
Strawberries, fresh	25
Eggplant	20
Fructose, granulated or liquid	20
Almonds, walnuts, hazelnuts	15
Artichoke	15
Asparagus	15
Broccoli	15
Brussels sprouts	15
Cabbages	15
Cauliflower	15
Celery	15
Cucumbers	15
Lettuce (all kinds)	15
Onions	15
Peanuts	15
Peppers (red or green)	15
Mung bean sprouts	15
Mushrooms	15
Soy beans (cooked)	15
Soy sprouts	15
Spinach	15
Zucchini	15
Avocado	10

MODIFYING FACTORS OF THE GLYCEMIC INDEX

A food's glycemic index can vary depending on several factors:

1) The type of carbohydrate—how much it has been commercially processed. If a food is highly refined, for example, the wheat endosperm has been removed and cracked (as is the case with white bread, white rice, white flour; or corn-on-the-cob versus cornflakes)— and it is likely to have a high GI and is therefore unhealthy. .

2) The fiber content—this is related to the above processing, but also related to the absorption process. The more fiber in a food, the slower it will be absorbed and the less effect it will have on blood-sugar levels, and hence, the lower its GI.

3) What else is in the meal—the more fat and protein, the slower the meal will be absorbed and the less the rise in blood-sugar levels and insulin response.

4) The cooking method—heating in oil is less healthy. Fried potatoes have a much higher GI than potatoes boiled in their skins.

5) Ripeness for fruits—a green banana has a lower GI than a ripe one.

This is why, when determining the GI values of some foods, studies have arrived at more-or-less different values. Therefore, the values given in the GI table may be somewhat different from other sources since they are averaged results.

I haven't listed many commercially prepared ready-to-eat foods since these differ greatly from one another depending on the manufacturer, ingredients, and additives, and their GIs are highly variable. However you can refer to my website, *www.montignac.com*, for more information.

RECOMMENDATION: Whenever you are able, eat food that is as close to its original state as possible—i.e. unprocessed, raw, or briefly cooked— because overcooking increases the GI of natural starch. This is why I recommend eating spaghetti *al dente*—Europeans have been doing it for centuries. Whole-wheat varieties are better as well, since they have more fiber. And adding vegetables to your pasta can add even more fiber.

Carefully analyze the ingredients of commercial ready-to-eat products, and watch out for undesirable additives, or ingredients such as sugar, modified starch, syrup (high-fructose corn or rice), and malt.

Choosing the Right Carbohydrates

All foods in the High Glycemic Index table (GI of 110–55) may cause blood-sugar levels to rise sharply, depending on what else you are eating during a meal. They are considered hyperglycemic because eating them triggers a high rise in glycemia (blood-sugar level). In the previous section, I explained how a high blood-sugar level is followed by high insulin secretion. A high blood-insulin level can lead to an increase in calories being converted to fat for storage, which may also cause weight gain.

On the other hand, carbohydrates in the Low (GI of 50–40) and Very Low (GI of 35–10) Glycemic Index tables are healthier, because they cause a steadier increase in blood-sugar levels than high glycemic foods. As a result, insulin production also remains low, and calories have less of a chance of being stored as fat. Instead, carbohydrates and fats are used as fuel by the body to produce energy. If total calories are in balance with calories burned (or expended), then weight gain is avoided. If the insulin level is low, the body is also encouraged to break down stored fats and to use them as fuel. This use of energy leads to weight loss when the calories expended are greater than those consumed.

What Carbs Do Americans Eat?

In the Low/Very Low Glycemic Index tables, there are three types of foods:

- whole grains (whole-grain bread, whole-grain pasta, brown rice)
- beans (lentils, dried beans, peas, chickpeas, soy beans)
- fruit and vegetables (green vegetables, salad, mushrooms, fruits)

We know that these foods were eaten in large quantities by our ancestors, especially by our parents and grandparents. Even 50 years ago in France, people ate a dish containing lentils, beans, or peas every other day. In Spain, lentils and chickpeas were on the menu almost every day.

Now, let's look at the High Glycemic Index table on pages 32–33. First of all, we can see that this column contains most of the foods used regularly in a modern diet: sugar, white flour products, white rice, corn, and potatoes. If we look at American food habits, in terms of the GI table, this will lead us to understand the problem of obesity in the US.

SUGAR

Americans consume the largest amount of sugar worldwide. According to the US Sugar Association and the USDA, Americans consume about 64 pounds of sugar, including all caloric sweeteners, a year. Of that number, about 29 pounds is in the form of sucrose, or sugar (GI 70). Sugar is metabolic enemy number one for Americans, since it is consumed in large quantities and is highly hyperglycemic. It adds a significant amount of calories, contributes to the obesity problem because of its high GI, and is often found in foods with high saturated-fat content.

WHITE FLOUR

White flour (GI 85) is used in the preparation of crackers, pizza, hot-dog and hamburger buns, sandwich bread, English muffins, hard rolls, bagels, sweet baked goods, and more. All these foods are often eaten several times a day. This diet is therefore very hyperglycemic.

POTATOES

Some people eat potatoes two to three times a day: hash browns at breakfast, French fries at lunch, and mashed potatoes at dinner. They are a classic American food. But unfortunately, they are a high glycemic food. Potatoes, mainly prepared as French fries, scalloped potatoes, and mashed potatoes, have a glycemic index (90 to 95) almost as high as glucose.

CORN

The corn that was once eaten by indigenous Americans was an old type of corn with a high-amylose (resistant-starch) and fiber content, which led to a low GI (35). Modern high-yield sweet corn, on the other hand, has a high

GI (65). This type of corn is usually grilled or boiled either on or off the cob. However, when it is transformed to make popcorn or cornflakes, the GI is increased even further, up to 85, which makes it hyperglycemic. Corn also shows up as high-fructose corn syrup, which is used as the sweetener in so many unhealthy beverages—sodas, juice drinks, punches—because it is very cheap.

RICE

In contrast to traditional Asiatic and Indian rices such as basmati, high-yield American rices have a relatively high GI (70). But when these are turned into instant or sticky rice, their GI rises even higher (90). They are also worse for your weight, because during the processing of the rice, the fiber content is removed, including the vitamins and minerals—which are now put back in during the so-called "fortification" process.

To sum it up, US food habits often lead to high blood-sugar levels. At the end of each meal, many Americans have a high blood-sugar level, which leads to higher insulin production and causes the storage of fat, rather than the use of food for energy.

What About Fats?

All types of fats are grouped together under the heading "lipids." After digestion, they are available to the body as fatty acids.

Traditionally, fat from animal sources and fat from vegetable sources have been distinguished from each other because it was assumed that the latter is healthier. Today we know that this is not the case. This is why it is preferable to categorize fat according to its chemical structure—this makes its nutritional pros and cons clearer.

Fats are essential to nutritional balance. They deliver energy that can be stored anytime and take part in numerous bodily functions. Fats control the formation of membranes, cells, and tissues, especially those of the nervous system. They also aid in the production of various hormones. If the wrong fats are eaten, they may increase cardiovascular risks factors and can lead to heart attack. Bad fats are also involved in weight gain.

Fats can be divided into four categories, depending on the types of fatty acids they contain:

SATURATED FATS

These are found mostly in beef, veal, lamb, fatty meats (bacon, sausage, salami, bologna, ribs, brisket, hot dogs) and full-fat dairy products, (ice cream, whole milk, cream, butter, cream cheese, and cheese). We know that saturated fats clog up the arteries and contribute to an increased risk of heart disease.

TRANS FATS

Trans fats are used mostly in processed foods such as cookies, donuts, crackers, chips, and many packaged products, to improve taste and shelf life. These are similar to polyunsaturated vegetable fats, but their chemical make-up is altered by industrial processing such as occurs when margarine is made, or during cooking. Trans fats have the same bad effects on the body as saturated fat. It is important to note that just because a food is labeled "trans free" does not mean that it is calorie free or low in saturated fat. So always check the nutrition label for saturated fat. If it has more than 3 grams of saturated fat, than the original "health" benefit is negated. Instead of using trans fats, some companies are debating a return to using tropical oils, such as coconut or palm oil.

MONOUNSATURATED FATS

The new 2005 Dietary Guidelines for Americans, issued by the USDA, encourage people to eat more healthy fats, but there is a lot of confusion about which fats are healthy and what types of foods people should eat. Substituting monounsaturated fats for saturated fats can lower the risk of heart disease by improving cholesterol levels. These healthier mononunsaturated fats are found in olive oil, canola oil–based products, avocados, and even certain nuts and nut butters, such as almonds and walnuts. In France, in addition to olive oil, we also use goose and duck fat for cooking, which is part of the so-called "French paradox." These fats (along with foie gras) seem to lower cardiovascular risk factors the same way olive oil does.

POLYUNSATURATED FATS

Polyunsaturated fats include omega-3 and omega-6 fatty acids. Omega-3 fatty acids have a number of health benefits, such as lowering the risk of heart disease by improving cholesterol levels, and have recently been touted as being good for your skin. These fats are found in fatty cold-water fish, mayonnaise, vegetable oils, flax seeds, and nuts. Food companies are also beginning to enrich foods with omega-3 fats, and supplements are also available. Eating omega-6 fats is important, because even though they are essential to your body's hormone regulation, the body does not make some of these essential fats, so they have to come from your diet. Mayonnaise, vegetable oils and spreads, and nuts all contain omega-6 fatty acids. Since most fats contain a combination of saturated, monos, and polys, it important to use the ones with the healthiest profile.

Most polyunsatured fats are not affected as much by insulin levels since they first have to be converted to saturated fatty acids before they can be stored in fatty tissue. Some fatty acids are almost never stored as fatty deposits, even when insulin is secreted, which is why they don't make you fat. This is the case with omega-3s. Some studies have actually shown that burning these fats consumes more energy than theys contain, thus leading to weight loss.

The Effect of Protein on Weight

There are two sources of protein: animal and vegetable. They complement one another. This is the reason why some types of vegetarian diets are problematic. Vegetable products contain much less protein than animal products. In addition, the body cannot absorb vegetable protein easily.

SOURCES OF PROTEIN	
Animal protein	meat, poultry, fish, eggs, seafood, dairy products
Vegetable protein	cereals, beans, seeds and nuts, algae

Since consuming protein does not directly lead to weight gain, it has been considered "neutral" for a long time and ignored. Yet protein can have a direct influence on weight. Nutritionists have long recommended that only 15% of total energy consumption should come from protein. However, too little protein consumption can hinder weight loss, while protein consumption of more than 15% can prevent weight gain and aid in losing weight, since eating more protein leads to a greater feeling of fullness.

Nutritional Balance

For half-a-century, nutritionists have maintained that an energy balance results when energy consumed at each meal consists of the following:

- 15% protein
- 30% fat
- 55% carbohydrates

This "pseudo balance" was shown graphically on the USDA Food Guide Pyramid (see page 20), officially recommended by public-health officials in many Western countries. Today, epidemiological studies show that this food pyramid has had significant impact on the increasing prevalence of obesity, type 2 diabetes, and heart and cardiovascular disease worldwide. The USDA pyramid is currently being revised.

The new nutritional balance recommended by the French Diet looks like this:

- 30% protein
- 30% fat (especially mono- and polyunsaturated)
- 40% carbohydrates (especially those with a low or very low glycemic index)

The categories of foods that you should eat, and which correspond to these percentages, are illustrated in the French Diet Food Pyramid, on the next page.

THE FRENCH DIET FOOD PYRAMID

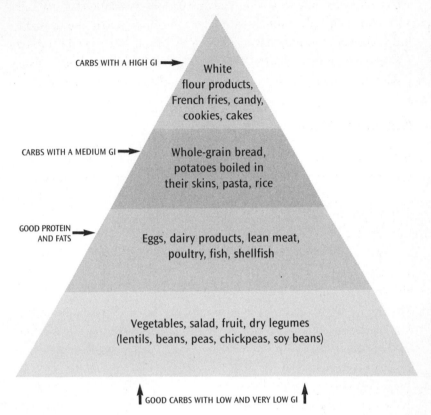

CARBS WITH A HIGH GI ➡ White flour products, French fries, candy, cookies, cakes

CARBS WITH A MEDIUM GI ➡ Whole-grain bread, potatoes boiled in their skins, pasta, rice

GOOD PROTEIN AND FATS ➡ Eggs, dairy products, lean meat, poultry, fish, shellfish

Vegetables, salad, fruit, dry legumes (lentils, beans, peas, chickpeas, soy beans)

⬆ GOOD CARBS WITH LOW AND VERY LOW GI ⬆

This balance does not have to be met at every meal as long as it is met on a daily basis.

Eating approximately 30% of protein a day on the French Diet—and only carbohydrates with low GIs—leads to a greater feeling of fullness. This feeling takes effect more quickly and lasts longer, which is why you can wait until the next meal without feeling hungry and are not driven to snack between meals.

4

Vive Le French Diet

THE FRENCH DIET IS NOT A DIET IN THE USUAL SENSE. A diet is generally understood to be a nutritional method based on eating limited quantities for a specified time. The French Diet is all about making a lifestyle change toward a balanced way of eating. It is based on choosing foods according to their macronutrients—carbohydrates, fats, and proteins—and their ability to initiate metabolic reactions that prevent weight gain, type 2 diabetes, and heart and cardiovascular disease.

The French Diet has helped hundreds of thousands of people to get their weight problems permanently under control. Their letters, and the positive feedback from hundreds of doctors all over the world, have been a constant source of encouragement to me.

About 85% of the people who have followed the rules of the French Diet have lost significant amounts of weight and most have kept it off. Those who have applied the method most successfully say it is not only simple and easy to follow, but it is has actually been enjoyable—to the point that it has reawakened their pleasure in eating, and eating well! Some people feel so good in Phase 1 (the weight-loss portion of the program) that they're in no particular hurry to move on to Phase 2 (weight maintenance).

In addition to losing weight and keeping it off, people have written to say that the French Diet has a few benefits they hadn't expected:

- the disappearance of gastrointestinal problems

- an improvement in physical and mental vigor, as well as less fatigue

- shorter and more recuperative periods of sleep

- greater resistance to illness, probably because the French Diet is rich in micronutrients (vitamins, minerals and trace elements)

Weight-Loss Studies

The principles behind the French Diet are not my discovery alone, although I was the first to make information about the glycemic index available to a wide readership in Europe. The glycemic index is the result of numerous scientific studies that have been published since the end of the 1970s as well as the experimental work I carried out with the help of many doctors and nutritionists from around the world.

THE BODY MASS INDEX (BMI) STUDY

In 1994, studies conducted by Dr. Anne Caupin and Dr. Hervé Robert, of France's Institut National de la Nutrition, initiated a study on 150 women between 18 and 68 years of age. The study was divided into three groups according to the women's BMI (see page 182): 32 women had a BMI under 24 (average weight); 80 women had a BMI between 24 and 29 (several pounds overweight); and 38 women had a BMI above 29 (obese). All the subjects of the study knew the principles of the French Diet, as a result either of reading my books or what they had been taught by their doctors.

Results at the End of 4 Months

BMI	Average weight lost	Weight lost (in percent)	Reduction of BMI	Reduction of BMI (in percent)
less than 24	12.06 lb	8.81%	2.11	9.2%
24 to 29	17.95 lb	11.86%	3.24	11.85%
30 to 40	29.48 lb	14.42%	5.09	14.55%

Results at the End of 12 Months

BMI	Average weight lost	Weight lost (in percent)	Reduction of BMI	Reduction of BMI (in percent)
less than 24	9.66 lb	6.74%	1.76	7.9%
24 to 29	17.95 lb	10.41%	3.00	10.9%
30 to 40	40.70 lb	19.77%	6.96	20.22%

As the above tables show, there was an average weight loss of 12 pounds within the less-than-24 group at the end of four months. At the end of a year, the body "found" its natural weight: Overall, average weight loss therefore stabilized at about 10 pounds. In the group with a BMI between 24 and 29, the subjects had lost an average 18 pounds at the end of four months, and achieved their ideal weight. In the group with a BMI between 30 and 40, the subjects had lost on average 30 pounds at the end of four months. At the end of a year, the average weight lost was more than 40 pounds. One of the conclusions of the study was that weight loss was progressive, even if the rate of loss slowed down as the body approached its ideal weight.

THE EFFECT OF A LOW-GI, LOW-FAT, HIGH-PROTEIN DIET ON ABDOMINALLY OBESE MEN

Professor Jean G. Dumesnil, a cardiologist at the Heart Institute of Laval University Hospital in Quebec, had been overweight for some time and was unable to slim down. One of his colleagues at the hospital recommended the French Diet to him and Dumesnil lost 46 pounds.

Another colleague, the nutritionist Professor Angelo Tremblay, was so intrigued by the results obtained by Professor Dumesnil that together they decided to undertake an independent study in 1997 to try and isolate the active parameters of the French Diet.

The authors of the study therefore compared the effects of three diets on a group of men about 47 years old, having a BMI of 28 and an average weight of 227 pounds.

During the first week, the group followed a low-fat diet based on the recommendations of the American Heart Association. During the second week, the group followed the French Diet. In the third week, they were given the same number of calories as they had eaten during the second week, but with the same macronutrient composition as in the first week.

While following the diets, all the participants were allowed to eat as much as they liked, although those following Diet 2 (the French Diet) were only allowed to eat carbohydrates with a low glycemic index.

Details of the nutritional characteristics of the three diets, taken as an average for the whole period of the study, are as follows:

Nutrient Breakdown of the Three Diets in the Laval Study

	Diet 1 (AHA)	Diet 2 (French)	Diet 3 (Composite)
Protein	15%	31%	16%
Fats	30%	32%	30%
Carbohydrates	55%	37%	54%

Diet 2 (the French Diet) gave the greatest feelings of fullness, compared to the two other diets, primarily because the subjects were allowed to eat only carbohydrates with a low glycemic index, as well as more protein (0.7 g per pound of body weight). If we compare the relative changes in weight from the three diets expressed as percentages, we'll find that:

- Diet 1 (American Heart Association) caused the subjects to increase weight by 0.2 %. As a result, they were even heavier at the end of the trial than they were at the beginning.

- Diet 3 (Composite), which had the same caloric content as Diet 2 (athough it placed no restriction on the GI of the carbohydrates eaten, and had a different distribution of basic nutrients, favoring carbohydrate intake), showed that weight loss over the period of the trial was confined to a mere 1.7% of initial body weight.

- The best results were obtained by Diet 2 (French), which produced a weight loss of 2.4% with respect to initial body weight (about 7 pounds in 6 days, based on a subject initially weighing 227 pounds).

The study also shows that the French Diet, which stresses the metabolic potential of food (especially the glycemic index of carbohydrates), causes, in a very short time, a positive modification of many metabolic parameters:

- lower glycemia (blood sugar) and insulin level during the day

- reduction in total cholesterol

- improvement of the ratio of total cholesterol to HDL cholesterol

- spectacular reduction of 35% in triglyceride levels

The results of this study were officially presented at the Eighth International Congress on Obesity, which took place in Paris in August 1998. Later they were published in the November 2001 issue of the *British Journal of Nutrition*.

The Principles Of The French Diet

The intent of the French Diet is to change eating habits in order to reach these goals:

- weight loss

- prevention of weight gain (keeping the weight off)

- prevention of type 2 diabetes

- reduction of the risk factors for heart disease

The French Diet is based on several principles. However, before you put them into action, it is important to be mentally prepared and to rid your mind of any outdated dietary dogma that may still be lurking there.

Now that we've learned there is no direct relationship between weight gain and the energy content of our meals, let us drive the term "calories" out of our minds. Let us no longer ask whether food, especially fats, are calorie-rich. Let us finally stop talking about "slow" and "fast" sugars, since we now know that these terms are useless. It is scientifically proven that they do not lead us to our desired goal. We should free ourselves from the misleading opinions about nutrition that have become part of our culture and are still being propagated by many traditional dietary experts and the media.

It is essential to select foods according to their nutritional value and the effects they have on metabolism. Carbohydrates with a low (less than 50) or very low (less than 35) glycemic index are preferred. Polyunsaturated omega-3 fatty acids and monounsaturated fatty acids are ideal; saturated fatty acids and trans fats should be eaten sparingly. Protein should be chosen according to its origins (vegetable or animal) and how it proportionally complements the rest of your meal. All of these requirements are made clear in the French Diet, which consists of two phases: weight loss and weight maintenance.

PHASE 1: WEIGHT LOSS

In Phase 1, you lose weight and regulate your pancreatic function. This stage takes three to six months, depending on your body's metabolism and the amount of extra weight you need to lose (it may take a bit longer for very overweight people). During this time you will learn to alter your dietary habits and to replace bad choices with healthy ones, for example choosing "good" carbohydrates and "good" fats. In the process, you will detoxify your body and restore its natural balance by putting fewer demands on your pancreas and thus giving it a chance to recover.

This phase is easy to follow since there are almost no limits on the quantities you can eat. Those of you who have have followed one low-calorie diet after another will be happy to hear that you can finally eat as much as you want to—like the French—yet still lose weight. Also, Phase 1 is easy to follow, whether you eat at home or dine out, so you don't have to worry about dropping your social life in order to drop pounds. Phase 1 meals contain plenty of fiber, vitamins, minerals, and trace elements, and, best of all, they are balanced and delicious.

PHASE 2: WEIGHT MAINTENANCE

Phase 2 is a continuation of Phase 1 and should be followed for the rest of your life—a pleasurable mandate because even though you'll still need to select carbs according to their GI, your food choices will be much broader than in Phase 1.

In both phases of the French Diet, no sacrifices have to be made. Each day, you will realize with great pleasure how filling and satisfying this new diet is.

5

Phase 1: Weight Loss

The Principles

P HASE 1 ISN'T JUST ABOUT LOSING WEIGHT—it's all about achieving an
equilibrium that you will be able to maintain for the rest of your life. It
starts with a detox program of sorts, which sounds a little austere, but you'll
soon find that regulating your pancreatic function, changing your eating
habits, and learning to replace bad carbohydrates and fats with good ones
actually feels remarkably cleansing and energizing. You will also be eating
some of the best food you've ever had and you will not feel deprived for a
minute. So please don't feel put off by the long lists of foods you shouldn't
eat during Phase 1. Remember: This is the French Diet after all, which means
that wonderful meals are de rigeur—they are not optional. Good food
should make you feel good, and that's what the French Diet is all about.

At the start of Phase 1 everyone wonders, quite naturally, how long it will
last. There is no standard answer to this question—the amount of time
depends on your body's sensitivity. The rhythm of weight loss can vary
widely from one person to the next. For some, weight loss happens very
rapidly at the beginning and then slows down. You have to be patient
and accept your own rhythm. I do suggest, however, that you follow
Phase 1 for at least three months to give your body time to adjust to a
new way of eating.

During the first week, record what you eat at meals. This will help you
keep track of the nutritional balance of your meals at all times and identify
eventual weak points. This is a very useful exercise and doesn't need to take
up much of your time. Jotting down a few notes about what you eat on a
regular basis can be a real eye-opener when you're trying to lose weight. Pay
attention to how often you eat foods that aren't good for you (and what they
are). Once you've identified your weak spots you can start addressing them
with the French Diet.

NEVER SKIP A MEAL

I do have a few strong opinions and a few rules, which should come as no
surprise, but I really do feel strongly about them, and they are all part of the
reason why the French Diet is so successful. Here's the most important
rule—three meals a day are absolutely required!

- a balanced breakfast
- a big lunch
- a light dinner

Skipping breakfast is a very bad idea. You won't lose weight by starving yourself. If you skip breakfast, your blood sugar drops, food cravings and hunger set in, and you end up overeating or eating too much of the wrong food. By "a balanced breakfast," I mean no sugary or fatty carbohydrates. Instead, I offer lots of recipes for delicious, easy-to-make egg dishes that don't skimp on flavor and will keep you going until lunchtime.

The idea of skipping lunch is just as bad as skipping breakfast, for all of the same reasons. And why should you forego lunch if you can eat as much as you like? In fact, if you follow the French Diet, lunch is the most important meal of the day, and it's the biggest, so start getting used to the idea of enjoying a delicious, completely satisfying meal at lunchtime.

Skipping dinner has fewer consequences but I strongly discourage it. You absolutely need three regular meals a day. Dinner is a lighter affair than lunch. However, if you follow my plan, but you can always have a between-meal snack—unless you opt to have four or five smaller meals. Some studies have shown that energy consumption and weight loss is higher when a given amount of food is divided between five meals, instead of three, but for this to work, you need a very high level of organization, as well as the time to carefully structure your meals. You can also say goodbye to snacking if you follow the five-meal plan. Personally, I prefer eating three delicious meals a day. Who has time to prepare five?

THE PROTEIN/CARB/FATS BALANCING ACT

The French Diet is composed of 30% protein, 30% fat, and 40% carbohydrates. Experience has shown that this balance can be achieved quite naturally if you follow the plan, and, especially, if you are careful to eat carbohydrates with a low glycemic index (GI). In fact, two studies have proven it: During the Dumesnil study (see pages 48–49), participants who followed the French Diet could eat whatever they liked. Dumesnil reported that without any coaching or instruction, the participants in the study chose foods that contained:

- 31% protein
- 32% fats
- 37% carbohydrates

Another study, conducted in 1994 by the CFRV (Centre Français de la Recherche sur les Vitamines), compared menus in the French Diet with foods naturally selected by the test group. Here again there was an astonishing similarity between the foods participants had opted to eat during the study and the menus proposed in the French Diet. The CFRV research resulted in the following daily dietary profile:

- 29.3% protein
- 31.2% fats
- 37% carbohydrates

It is interesting to note that participants in the CFRV study also chose to eat foods that are naturally high in fiber. In fact 24.4% of the carbohydrates they ate contained fiber. The French Diet, of course, also includes fiber because it does not convert to glucose and, consequently, does not raise your blood-sugar level. Fiber reduces the entry of glucose into the bloodstream. This, in turn, reduces the blood-sugar spikes that trigger insulin production and encourage the body to make and store fat. In other words, including fiber in your diet is a fantastic way to get the most out of your food while you are trying to lose weight. You will feel full longer and experience fewer cravings.

Carbs to Avoid in Phase I

Since the end of the second half of the 20th century in America, mass-produced, highly processed foods have found their way into people's kitchens and onto their plates, often three times a day. These include modified starches—substances created during the chemical processing of starches, and which increase the thickening (gelatinization) of a product. Unfortunately, overprocessed foods are largely responsible for all the extra weight people carry around, because they contain bad carbohydrates and fats, as well as additives and preservatives. Overprocessing dangerously reduces the important fiber content of these foods. See pages 58–59 for lists of the foods that should be avoided in Phase I.

TRANSLATING NUTRIENTS INTO MEALS

It is important to consume the right balance of nutrients over the course of a day, taking into account the total of all meals consumed. This means you do not have to carefully monitor every single meal. For example, you can eat more carbohydrates (as long as they are low GI) at breakfast and dinner and fewer at lunch, where you eat more protein and fat. For example:

Breakfast   Fresh fruit
Whole-wheatbread
Unsweetened jam

Lunch   Caesar salad
(without croutons)
T-bone steak

Dinner   Spaghetti al dente
Tomato sauce

In order for proteins, fats, and carbohydrates to be balanced according to these principles, carbohydrates should have a maximum GI of 35.

For example:chicken breast with white beans contains:

- protein: in the meat of the chicken breast
- fat: in the chicken breast and the skin
- carbohydrates: in the white beans (GI 30)

If a meal consists of a carbohydrate with a low glycemic index (GI between 35 and 50), such as spaghetti, basmati rice, or sweet potatoes, any kind of protein is a good complement. However, be aware that the only kind of fats that should be eaten during Phase 1 are omega-3 fatty acids, which can be found in fish. For example: brown rice with salmon contains:

- protein: in the salmon
- fat: in the salmon
- carbohydrates: in the brown rice (GI 50)

CARBS TO AVOID IN PHASE 1

White flour in all its forms:	Sugar, contained in:	Potatoes in all forms, especially:	White rice of western origin: (see Note)	Modified starches in overprocessed foods, especially:
white bread	sodas	French fries	white long-grain rice	canned foods of all kinds
baked goods (including breads, muffins, and waffles)	juices	roasted potatoes	White short-grain rice	ready-made sauces
baked goods made with white semolina flour	baked goods (including breads, muffins, and waffles)	mashed potatoes		store-bought mayonnaise
cookies	cookies	scalloped potatoes		store-bought desserts
cakes	cakes	potato chips		frozen dairy products
crackers	breakfast cereals			
sandwiches	granola/ breakfast bars			
pizza	milk-chocolate bars and other chocolate candy			
cereal flakes	ice cream, hard candy, most canned goods, and prepackaged meals			

NOTE: Any rice with a GI higher than that of original Indian and Asian rice types should be avoided in Phase 1. Western rices should be avoided in Phase 1 because they are so overprocessed that they substantially raise the glycemic level of a meal. Indian and Asian rices are preferable because the grains are whole and include the all-important fiber, which is beneficial to your digestive system as the starches break down.

The following commercially processed substances should also be avoided:

- all types of syrups (malt and high-fructose corn syrups)

- dextrin and maltodextrin (thickening agents usually made from cornstarch, found in creams, beer, baked goods, candy, gravy, pie fillings, poultry products, puddings, and soups)

- other amylopectins (the insoluble part of starches), the most common thickening agents used by the food industry. You can even find them in infant milk formula, and in all baby food that comes in jars. You will also find them in most ready-to-eat dishes, sauces, instant soups, and ice cream—a real disaster, since their GI is 100!

FATS TO AVOID IN PHASE I

You should try to eliminate highly saturated fats from your diet altogether, but in Phase 1, choose the leanest cuts of meat, and avoid items such as fatty sausages, bacon, hot dogs, butter, whole-milk products, and high-fat cheeses such as American Swiss, cheddar, and brie. Similarly, trans fats should be avoided—including margarine, commercially baked goods, and chips.

Please see pages 39–41 for a full discussion on these bad fats, as well as the good fats you should be eating and should continue to eat through Phase II and beyond—monounsaturated fats such as olive oil and goose fat, and polyunsatured omega-3 and omega-6 fatty acids found in fish, nuts, and seeds.

Phase 1 Basics

Before getting into breakfast, lunch, and dinner, I have outlined the basic do's and don'ts of the French Diet:

WATER

While you are following the French Diet, it is a good idea to drink lots of water—carbonated or uncarbonated. Some people find that drinking carbonated water gives them gas. If this is the case, you should avoid drinking it. Others are convinced that carbonated water promotes digestion. This is entirely possible.

BEVERAGES

Black tea and all herbal teas can be enjoyed, but only when they are drunk without sugar. All refreshments with added sugar such as soft drinks, iced tea, and industrially produced fruit juices are to be avoided. You can have coffee for breakfast, but make it half decaf and half regular.

MILK

If skim milk agrees with you, you can drink it in moderation. Even though milk sugar (lactose) has a low GI, drinking too much of it may increase your insulin secretion.

BREAD

All bread, even whole-grain bread, has a glycemic index of over 35. This is why it should be banned from the menu during Phase 1 if the meal contains fats other than omega-3 fatty acids (see page 41 for a list of these). You must therefore learn to do without bread. If you like cheese or foie gras, you can have a salad with it instead of bread. When you really have an urge to eat some cheese, foie gras, tapenade, or guacamole on something, use a slice of fiber-rich, whole-grain crispbread with a minimum 20% fiber content in place of ordinary bread. But be sure to limit yourself to one or two slices at the very most.

HERBS, SPICES, AND COOKING/FLAVORING INGREDIENTS

Herbs, spices, and various condiments and oils can lend a great deal of flavor and texture to food without adding a lot of bad fats and sugar—if you're careful. As with any other food, however, moderation is key.

For example, Béarnaise and hollandaise sauce, crème fraîche, homemade mayonnaise, mustard (other than Dijon), pepper, and salt can be used in small quantities, while béchamel sauce, along with commercially prepared mayonnaise, should be avoided altogether. Oils made from peanuts, hazelnuts, olives, sunflower seeds, grape seeds, and walnuts can be used in reasonable quantities, but don't overdo them. Avoid palm oil. Also forbidden are two staples you will have to permanently forego if you are serious about losing weight: sugar and tomato ketchup (which is loaded with sugar). Other forbidden items are corn and potato starch, as well as soup- and sauce-thickening agents such as flour roux (which combines fat and flour). Caramel flavoring is off the "can have" list, too, because of the sugar content. Homemade dressings such as vinaigrette and Dijon mustard, however, can be used in reasonable quantities.

And you may enjoy various garnishes in reasonable quantities, too—for example: basil, bay leaves, chives, cinnamon, dill, parsley, savory, mint, tarragon, and thyme. Don't be shy about using garlic, onions, and shallots in moderation, too.

Salt consumption must be kept to a minimum because it can lead to high blood pressure and water retention, especially in women. The sodium in salt also plays a role in how glucose is metabolized. A reduction in salt consumption (or even giving it up completely) can lead to a reduction in the absorption of glucose. This prevents a rise in your blood-sugar level, and thus reduces weight gain. Flavor enhancers such as soy sauce and celery salt (as opposed to table salt), and garnishes that include pickles (other than sweet varieties) can be used in moderation as well. If you can't envision life without black and green olives, you don't have to! They're on the list of good things to enjoy in reasonable quantities, along with olive tapenade.

LET THEM EAT CHOCOLATE AND DESSERT—AND DRINK WINE!

Chocolate

In Phase 1 you can eat one or two pieces of dark chocolate with 70% cacao every now and then for dessert, but moderation is the key. You might wonder how chocolate can be allowed at all in the French Diet, given its sugar content. Dark chocolate with a minimum cacao content of 70% has a low glycemic index (25). This type of chocolate does contain 25% to 29% sugar, but it also contains many soluble fibers that neutralize the increase in blood-sugar levels caused by sugar. This is why, when the rise in blood sugar is seen in total, the mixture of sugar and fiber in the cacao leads to a very low rise. You may also be surprised that the French Diet champions chocolate even though it has a high saturated-fat content. Dr. Ancel Keys, a University of Minnesota public-health scientist who discovered that saturated fat was a major cause of heart disease, also found that the saturated fats of chocolate (made up of stearic acid) are turned into oleic acid during digestion. This is the same type of fat found in olive oil. Seventy percent of the fatty acids absorbed into the blood after eating chocolate are monounsaturated fatty acids. It follows that dark chocolate with 70% cacao content can help in lowering cholesterol and blood sugar.

Wine

During Phase 1 you can certainly drink a glass of wine at the end of a meal, but don't drink more than one because it will hinder weight loss. Also, it is better to drink wine at the end of a meal.

Avoid drinking wine on an empty stomach because the alcohol goes more rapidly into your blood. For this reason, you should always eat something before having a glass of wine or an aperitif (champagne is the only permitted aperitif).

Baked Goods/Desserts

Perhaps you are a little worried that that if you go on the French Diet you will never be able to enjoy baked goods and other treats again. Rest assured—this is not the case. What I condemn in so many baked goods are their bad carbohydrates (in the form of flour and sugar), and their bad fats (such as butter and margarine). The French Diet replaces sugar with any substitute that has a neutral GI, and flour can either be replaced with ground almonds or hazelnuts, or it can be left out completely. And, in most cases, it can be replaced with olive oil, if fat is needed. Desserts that you can eat while you are on the French Diet are made from the following ingredients:

- fruit or fruit compote
- eggs
- quark or yogurt
- ground almonds or hazelnuts
- sugar substitute or low-GI fructose (20 GI or less)
- milk
- dark chocolate with a minimum of 70% cacao content

Take a look at the dessert recipes in this book and you'll see some very attractive options for low GI desserts. There's absolutely no reason why you can't have your cake and eat it too!

Phase 1 Protein Breakfast

In the morning, after about ten hours without nourishment, your body needs glucose. For this reason, it is important to be selective about the kind of carbohydrates you eat at breakfast. Since the blood-sugar level tends to peak in the morning, however, you should also avoid excess fats such as those found in cheese, eggs, butter, cream, and other whole-milk products if possible. These fats are stored as a result of the high insulin response.

Protein, on the other hand, is an excellent choice for breakfast. You can eat it in the form of skim-milk products, ham with the fat removed, or, even better, thin slices of chicken or turkey breast with a fat content of less than 2%. It is also permissible to eat fish such as tuna, whitefish, and salmon (including smoked salmon). You can also follow a southern Spanish tradition of eating toasted whole-grain bread drizzled with olive oil. Olive oil can help lower the blood-sugar level.

Phase 1 Carbohydrate Breakfast

Of all the Phase 1 breakfasts, this is probably the most popular, not only because it is the easiest to prepare but because it provides the best available energy in the morning.

After eating some fresh fruit you can also choose to have a portion of high-fiber bread (such as whole wheat) with unsweetened jam or a serving of whole-grain cereal. On the next page is a chart of recommended and acceptable foods for a Phase 1 carbohydrate breakfast, as well as forbidden options.

RECOMMENDED, ACCEPTABLE, AND FORBIDDEN PHASE I CARB BREAKFASTS

	Recommended	Acceptable	Forbidden
FRESH FRUIT	apples cherries grapefruit kiwis lemons nectarines oranges peaches pears plums raspberries strawberries	bananas, light green plantains mangoes papayas pineapples	bananas, very ripe canned fruit, sugar added
FRESH VEGETABLES/ SALADS	carrots, raw cucumbers green lentil puree hummus mushrooms onions peppers salad tomatoes		
BREAD, COOKIES, CAKES, PASTRIES, AND CANDIES	fiber-rich whole-grain crispbread, minimum 20% fiber content pumpernickel bread whole-grain bread, 100%	black bread whole-grain bagel whole-grain bread whole-grain bread, toasted whole-grain cookies, without sugar whole-grain roll whole-grain rye bread, finely ground	biscotti cookies croissants honey ladyfingers maple syrup muffins sugar waffles white bread white-bread toast yeast-risen pastry

	Recommended	Acceptable	Forbidden
CEREAL FLAKES AND YEAST	brewer's yeast oat bran wheat sprouts whole-grain flakes, without sugar	muesli, without sugar oat flakes wheat bran	cereal flakes, with sugar cornflakes puffed corn puffed rice
JAMS	applesauce, without sugar fruit spread, without sugar unsweetened jam	jam with fructose hazelnut spread, without sugar	hazelnut spread, with sugar jams/jellies, with sugar
SOURCES OF PROTEIN	chicken breast, 2% fat low-fat smooth cottage cheese low-fat curd-style cottage cheese herring mackerel or sardines, fresh or smoked plain soy yogurt quark salmon, fresh or smoked tuna fish in water low-fat turkey breast low-fat yogurt	reduced-fat smooth cottage cheese reduced-fat curd-style cottage cheese reduced-fat ham quark reduced-fat milk	bacon butter cheese cottage cheese, whole-fat cream cream yogurt curd-style cottage cheese, 20% fat eggs boiled ham margarine quark salami sausages soy yogurt, with sugar whole milk whole-milk yogurt with sugar yogurt with fruit and sugar (commercially prepared) cocoa beverages made with whole-milk and sugar (commercial products) coffee, strong
DRINKS	cocoa, minimum 70% cacao coffee, decaffeinated milk, 1% soy milk tea, black tea, fruit tea, green tea, herbal	coffee, half decaf and half regular fruit juice, freshly squeezed milk, reduced-fat vegetable juice, freshly-pressed	drinks with alcohol fruit juices, with sugar soft drinks

FRUIT JUICES

When you drink fruit juices right after getting up in the morning, your blood-sugar level increases sharply, even when the juice is freshly squeezed. This is why it is better to avoid fruit juices entirely. If you really want to drink fruit juice, then drink it only after breakfast, when it will have less of an affect on your blood-sugar level. It is certainly inadvisable to drink commercially prepared artificial fruit juices from bottles, cans, or boxes, even when no sugar has been added, not only because they have a higher GI, but because they lack fresh vitamins.

FRUIT

Some people have very delicate digestive systems. When they eat fruit during or after a meal, it can sometimes ferment and cause digestive discomforts such as gas and bloating. If you have a sensitive digestive system, eat fresh fruit before a meal whenever possible, and wait 15 minutes before eating anything else. This allows the fruit to be digested separately from other foods. People whose systems are less sensitive can eat fruit during or after a meal. For example, you can add fresh fruit to your whole-grain cereal at breakfast.

BREAD

The only bread I recommend is 100% whole-grain bread. This marvelous "real" bread is called "integral" bread in Europe, and it is made from stone-ground whole-grain flour and leavened with natural sourdough yeast. With the advent of artisan bakeries in the US, and a new interest in real "Old World" breads that are handmade loaf by loaf, using only the best ingredients and baking methods, real whole-grain bread can now be found with greater regularity in bakeries, organic food stores, health-food stores, gourmet food shops (including those online) and other specialty food stores.

In France, bread is an institution and is taken very seriously, not only because it has real food value, but because each hand-crafted loaf has its own distinctive shape, texture, and taste, ranging in flavor from sweet and mild to pungent and rustic.

You should toast 100% whole-grain bread because it slightly lowers the glycemic index. As an alternative, you can buy pumpernickel, which is made from rye meal. Be careful, though, because some manufacturers add sugar or fat. Usually these are in small quantities, and within the tolerance zone, so they should be good options for Phase 1. Whole-grain crispbread with a fiber-rich content of 20% to 25% is also recommended.

On all bread and crispbread types, you can spread reduced-fat cottage cheese or reduced-fat curd-style cottage cheese with a maximum of 2% to 3% fat. You can also top the bread with a slice of turkey or white chicken meat, lots of cucumber and tomato slices, and lettuce.

TEA, COFFEE, AND HOT CHOCOLATE

Drinking strong coffee during Phase 1 is not recommended since coffee can increase insulin production in some overweight people (a result of diets they've followed in the past). This is why you should make it a habit to drink decaffeinated coffee or, at most, a mix of caffeinated and decaffeinated coffee.

There are no restrictions on tea, even though it contains a bit of caffeine. However, you should be careful about buying commercial cocoa. Most hot cocoa mixes contain sugar and starches—especially the ones that are marketed to children. Buy unsweetened cocoa powder instead, and sweeten the beverage with a bit of fruit sugar only as needed.

CEREALS AND CEREAL PRODUCTS

This category is deceptive, because for the past 50 years, a variety of troubling industrial products have claimed to promote children's health behind the term "cereal." The amount of sugar in most of these products is staggering. All industrially produced or processed cereal flakes, cornflakes, wheat flakes, puffed rice, and puffed wheat should be banned from the menu since they have a hyperglycemic effect.

Acceptable are whole-grain cereal flakes such as wheat, barley, and, above all, oats. They should be eaten cold, with skim milk, low-fat yogurt, quark, low-fat cottage cheese, or low-fat curd-style cottage cheese, and can be sweetened as needed with a sugar-free fruit spread.

Avoid instant oatmeal, which has less fiber and more bad carbs than the kind of oatmeal that requires cooking. Be careful not to overcook oatmeal, which, although it is made from natural oats, can become gelatinous when cooked. This causes its glycemic index to increase and you lose the excellent dietary value of this food. Cook oatmeal for just a few minutes, and use skim milk and a sugar substitute instead of sugar. The coarser the oatmeal, the better it is for you.

Protein-Fat Breakfast

This type of breakfast is similar to a classic English breakfast that consists of bacon and eggs. It can also include other meats such as ham, steak, and sausage, as well as cheese or fish. This type of breakfast can be eaten now and then within the framework of the French Diet, but it does contain large quantities of saturated fats, so this variation should be excluded at the outset by anyone who has high cholesterol. When you are away from home and breakfasting at a hotel, for example, a protein-fat breakfast is often the most sensible choice since the possibility of finding good carbohydrates can be a challenge.

If you eat this type of breakfast, which is made up primarily of protein and fat, you should avoid every form of carbohydrate with the exception of apples and other carbohydrates with a low glycemic index.

PROTEIN-FAT BREAKFAST

	Recommended	Acceptable	Forbidden
FOODS	bacon cheese (low-fat cottage cheese, low-fat hard cheese) eggs (hard-boiled, fried, omelet, scrambled) fish, such as smoked salmon ham (cooked or cured)	almonds apples berries broccoli mushrooms nuts oranges peanuts tomatoes	bananas biscotti cereal flakes croissant (plain or chocolate) honey jams ladyfingers maple syrup potatoes white bread whole-grain bread yeast-risen pastries and cakes
BEVERAGES	decaf coffee green tea herbal tea milk, skim or reduced-fat	coffee, weak tea, black, weak whole milk	cocoa coffee, strong

MIDMORNING SNACKS

When your breakfast consists mainly of carbs with a high GI (white flour and products containing sugar), there is a high likelihood that you will become hungry before it's time for lunch. This is why so many people have the urge to snack between meals. But you wouldn't feel any hunger if you ate only carbs that have a low glycemic index—especially when they are eaten with protein foods such as reduced-fat cheese, chicken or turkey breast, and salmon—because foods containing protein cause the feeling of fullness to last longer. If you still want to eat a midmorning snack, I recommend foods that stave off hunger without dramatically affecting your blood-sugar level.

RECOMMENDED SNACKS:

- an apple
- plain yogurt
- a piece of hard cheese
- raw vegetables such as carrots, celery, cucumbers, peppers, and tomatoes

Phase 1 Lunch: At Work or On the Go

At lunch you must follow, without fail, the most important principle of the French Diet. Here's the rule: The carbohydrates you eat with this meal must have a glycemic index of 35 or below, in order to keep your blood sugar and insulin response as low as possible. Just as at breakfast, there is no quantity restriction, but you should eat enough to experience a pleasant feeling of fullness.

In the French Diet, lunch is, ideally, the most important meal of the day and therefore consists of the classic European first course (appetizer), main course, and dessert. Unfortunately not all of us are as lucky as about 70% of the French, Italians, and Spanish people who are able to eat lunch at home. And for people who don't have access to a cafeteria at work, the only options are to bring your own food or buy it from a local restaurant. There's plenty of fast food and items you can buy from street vendors, if the area around your workplace has them, but let's investigate a few of the drawbacks of some of these options.

DELI-BOUGHT SANDWICHES, HAMBURGERS, AND HOT DOGS

These foods should be scrupulously avoided since they are based on white-flour breads, a carbohydrate with a high or very high glycemic index. On top of this, most sandwiches, hot dogs, and hamburgers are eaten together with bad fats (saturated or polyunsaturated trans fatty acids) that are found in cold-cut meats like bologna, olive loaf, boiled ham, processed turkey loafs, and accompanying condiments. They also contain a large amount of sugar. It does not help much if you eat a deli-bought "whole-grain sandwich." Too often, these are just well-marketed products designed to deceive the health-conscious customer (although some high-end gourmet bakeries and markets may make sandwiches with fresh stone-ground whole-wheat bread). Industrially produced whole-grain bread contains little fiber and just as much bad fat and sugar as white bread. And its glycemic index approaches that of white bread, as well. For these reasons, the best alternative is to eat a homemade sandwich for lunch. Use 100% whole-grain bread, black bread, or pumpernickel. The advantage is that the many fibers in these types of breads help reduce the total glycemic content of the sandwich.

Bad fats such as butter, margarine, and those found in fatty sausage should be avoided at all costs. The only fats permitted are olive oil and fish fat. If you eat meat, it should not contain more than 4% fat.

ACCEPTABLE INGREDIENTS FOR SANDWICH MADE WITH 100% WHOLE-GRAIN BREAD

Vegetables	Spreads and Condiments	Meat, Poultry, Fish
raw carrots	cheese, reduced-fat	chicken breast, grilled
cucumbers	cottage cheese, low-fat smooth	cured ham, fat removed
lettuce	cottage cheese, low-fat curd-style	herring
mushrooms	quark	mackerel or sardine fillets, smoked
onions	yogurt, reduced-fat	roast beef, lean, trimmed of fat
peppers	hummus	salmon, smoked, poached, or grilled
tomatoes	Dijon mustard	tuna, fresh grilled, or tuna fish packed in water or vegetable oil
		turkey breast

Along with, or instead of, a sandwich made from the ingredients listed above, you can also bring a salad for your lunch. In it you can include: lettuce, grated carrot, pepper, cucumber, tomato, and zucchini, as well as chicken, turkey, tuna, and salmon. If you eat only salad and no bread, you can add Gruyère, feta, and mozzarella cheese. If you want to dressing to your salad, be sure to use homemade salad dressing made from olive oil and vinegar (see page 144), because commercially prepared salad dressings usually contain sugar or glucose.

PIZZA

From the French Diet point of view, pizza has only one disadvantage—its white-flour crust and fairly high glycemic index. By comparison, pizza toppings are usually more acceptable. I have provided a recipe for pizza that conforms to the French Diet (see page 138), using a pizza crust with flour that has a low glycemic index.

SALAD BAR

More and more salad bars are popping up in restaurants, company cafeterias, and food stores, including fast-food chains. By now you've probably internalized the general principles of the French Diet, so you'll undoubtedly make the right choices the next time you're choosing foods from the salad bar. The below table provides a quick reference list.

RECOMMENDED FOODS TO CHOOSE AT A SALAD BAR

Vegetables	Eggs and Cheese	Meat, Poultry, Fish, Tofu	Fruit
alfalfa sprouts	eggs, hard-boiled	chicken breast, grilled	blackberries
artichokes	cottage cheese, low-fat	crab	blueberries
asparagus		ham, cured	raspberries
avocados	feta	roast beef, lean, trimmed of fat	strawberries
bean sprouts	mozzarella, low-fat		
Boston lettuce		salmon, smoked, poached, or grilled	
brussels sprouts		tofu	
cabbage			
carrots, raw		tuna, fresh grilled, or plain tuna fish (no mayonnaise)	
cauliflower		turkey breast	
celery			
chickpeas			
cucumbers			
eggplant			
endive			
escarole			
green beans			
lentils			
mesclun (field greens)			
mushrooms			
olives (black/green)			
peas			
peppers			
radishes			
romaine lettuce			
sauerkraut			
soy-bean sprouts			
tomatoes			
zucchini			

NOTE: All of the vegetables in this list can be eaten raw or steamed briefly (to keep the GI low), except for carrots, which should always be eaten raw.

Even though a salad bar can seem like the land of milk and honey when you're on the French Diet, there are some hidden perils. Try to avoid the following traps:

- salads that contain potatoes, corn, or croutons
- deli (or lunch) meats containing saturated fat, modified starch, sugar, corn syrup, and various additives
- foods such as hot dogs, lunch meats, and meat spreads (i.e. liverwust) that might contain starch or flour
- quiches and toasted bread made from white flour

You would probably like to know whether or not you are allowed to eat pasta from the salad bar. Avoid all warm pasta, since its glycemic index is still too high for Phase 1. The only exception is spaghetti, which can be eaten only if it is cold, i.e. in a salad (without mayonnaise). Its glycemic index in this form is relatively low, close to 35.

If you can't finish a meal without a sweet taste and want to have a dessert other than berries (which should be your first choice), you can have one to three squares of dark chocolate (as long as it contains 70% cacao or more) together with a couple of almonds or hazelnuts.

Phase 1 Four-Course Lunch: The Big Meal Of The Day

When you're eating out in a restaurant, and are in quandary about what to order, think about the traditional foods of Mediterranean countries such as France, Italy, Spain, Portugal, or Greece, and carefully select a complete menu consisting of the following courses:

- appetizer—a green salad
- main course—fish or lean meat
- side dish—lots of vegetables
- dessert—low-fat cheese or fruit

On the next few pages are tables of guidelines to help you chart your lunch courses. And when ordering a salad in a restaurant, always ask for it without croutons. The recipe section has some great ideas for lunch dishes (pages 115–53) if you have a little more time to enjoy a homemade meal.

LUNCH: APPETIZERS

The items in the recommended column are either fresh raw vegetables or cooked vegetables served cold as a starter. For instance in any restaurant, entrées on the menu might include:

- Leeks or asparagus served with French vinaigrette—the vegetables have been cooked first and then cooled.

- Tomato salad—the tomatoes are usually sliced and served with vinaigrette. Mozzarella cheese, as well as eggs or even shrimp may be added

- Lentil salad—the lentils are cooked, chilled, and served with vinaigrette.

Sounds good, doesn't it? I can't tell you how many slim French women I've seen tucking into one of these refreshing appetizers as a prelude to a hearty, completely satisfying meal.

Since lunch should be a "protein-fat, very-low-GI carb" meal à la French Diet, all foods listed in column 1 are either very low carbs (GI 35 and below), or protein and fat.

Column 2 lists foods that are considered borderline. The GI for carbs in this column are between 35 and 40 (as in the case of cold pasta).

Column 3 lists obvious no-nos.

However, you'll notice that there are some protein-fat foods in column 2 that contain either a little sugar or starch or a portion of saturated or trans fat (paté for instance). I consider the inclusion of this delectable food a minor dietary transgression—as long as you promise not to eat it too often or in large quantities.

No bread should be eaten before or during this meal. Even if the restaurant serves homemade pumpernickel rolls or whole-grain crispbread, don't order them: Remember, this Phase I "protein-fat lunch" excludes any carbs over 40 on the glycemic index.

PHASE I RECOMMENDED, ACCEPTABLE, AND FORBIDDEN
APPETIZER FOODS FOR LUNCH

	Recommended	Acceptable	Forbidden
FRUITS AND VEGETABLES, GRAINS, CARBS, AND STARCHES	apples artichokes asparagus avocados Boston lettuce beans, dried broccoli cabbage carrots, raw cauliflower chicory chickpeas cucumbers dandelion leaves eggplant green beans leeks endive escarole hearts of palm lentils mushrooms olives (black/green) peas peppers radishes romaine lettuce tomatoes watercress zucchini	grapefruit melons (cantaloupe/honeydew)* spaghetti, cold watermelon*	bread corn crackers donuts pancakes, crêpes pizza potatoes puff pastry quiche rice soufflé toast

* NOTE: Although they have a high GI, these foods are acceptable because the amount of carbohydrate is so low that its effect on the blood sugar is negligible.

	Recommended	Acceptable	Forbidden
FISH AND SHELLFISH	anchovies calamari (squid) caviar clams crab fish soup (made without flour and sugar) herring lobster mackerel mussels octopus oysters red snapper salmon (poached, grilled, or smoked) sardines scallops sea bass shrimp/prawns sole tuna		
EGGS, SOUPS & RELISH	eggs benedict (light on the sauce) eggs, hard-boiled or scrambled egg salad gazpacho vegetable soup	homemade mayonnaise mustard	sweet pickles
MEAT	chicken liver confit duck-liver paté foie-gras (goose-liver paté) lean cooked or cured ham slab bacon snails (escargots)	bacon hard sausage liverwurst pork liver paté, smooth and country-style	fatty sausage
CHEESE	cheddar feta goat cheese, warm Gruyère mozzarella		

LUNCH: ENTRÉE

For your main dish, it is best to get the simplest preparation without heavy sauces, which often contain large amounts of sugar (especially ketchup and cocktail sauces). Please note the following imporant rules:
- For meat, do not eat fatty parts.
- Do not eat poultry skin.
- Make sure to tell your server that you do not want accompanying potatoes, which often come automatically with many dishes.

The following food products should not be eaten in conjunction with any of the other foods in the below table:
- bread and bread coating
- butter
- crackers
- toast

PHASE I RECOMMENDED, ACCEPTABLE, AND FORBIDDEN ENTRÉES FOR LUNCH

	Recommended		Acceptable
MEATS	beef buffalo lamb pork	rabbit veal venison	bacon
FISH (all fish is acceptable; these are some common offerings)	cod flounder herring mackerel perch red snapper salmon	sardines sea bass sole swordfish trout tuna whiting	
POULTRY (with skin removed)	capon chicken cornish game hen duck goose	ostrich pheasant quail turkey	
EGGS	Omelet with cheese, diced ham, or mushrooms		

LUNCH: SIDE DISHES

Fibrous vegetables are your best choice for a side dish, and there is an almost limitless list of recommended choices. Steer clear of bread, potatoes, noodles, and rice!

PHASE I RECOMMENDED, ACCEPTABLE, AND FORBIDDEN SIDES DISHES FOR LUNCH

Recommended	Acceptable	Forbidden
artichokes	carrots, cooked*	bread
asparagus	field (split) peas, peeled	bulgur wheat
broccoli	acorn squash	chestnuts
cabbage	pumpkin	couscous
cauliflower	lentils, brown	crackers
celery	red beans	egg noodles
dried beans	white turnips*	French fries
endive		pasta
fava beans		potatoes, boiled, mashed, roasted, scalloped
chickory		
eggplant		rice
garlic		toast
green beans		wheat semolina
lentils		
mushrooms		
onions		
peppers		
salsify		
sauerkraut		
sorrel		
spinach		
swiss chard		
tomatoes		
white beans		
zucchini		

* NOTE: Although they have a high GI, these foods are acceptable because the amount of carbohydrate in them is so low that its effect on blood sugar is negligible.

PHASE 1 LUNCH: DESSERT

As with breakfast, berries are highly recommended for dessert. But you can also have chocolate! Dark chocolate with a minimum cacao content of 70% has a low glycemic index (25).

PHASE I RECOMMENDED, ACCEPTABLE, AND FORBIDDEN DESSERTS FOR LUNCH

Recommended	Acceptable	Forbidden
aged cheese	chocolate fondue made with 70% cacao, without sugar or flour	bread
curd-style cottage cheese		crackers
Apple-Nut Torte without sugar or flour (see recipe, page 176),	Chocolate Mousse, made with dark chocolate with a minimum of 70% cacao without extra sugar (see recipe, page 178)	cookies
		custard, with sugar
		fruit baked with pastry
baked fruit of any kind (except bananas), particularly apple	raw fruit of any kind, except bananas	puddings (including rice pudding)
pears poached in wine, without sugar		bananas, ripe
raspberries		quark, with sugar
strawberries		yogurt with fruit or sugar
quark		
plain yogurt		

Dinner Phase I

Dinner differs from lunch in two ways: It is usually eaten at home and it is often the only decent meal of the day, since lunch is usually either a very hurried affair or, worse, it is skipped altogether (usually because of work). Dinner is frequently the only meal eaten with family and friends, and the temptation is huge, therefore, to eat too much. According to the French Diet's weight-reduction plan, however, this meal should be the light one.

If you are eating away from home as someone's guest or at a restaurant, it calls for a certain amount of discipline to remain true to the principles of the French Diet. But even this obstacle can be overcome if you heed the following dinner guidelines.

Choose to follow either the protein-fat, very-low-GI-carb formula or the carb-protein formula we saw in the lunch section. Just make it a bit smaller than lunch—as described below:

PROTEIN-FAT VERY LOW-GI-CARB MEAL

This dinner has the same structure as most lunches (i.e. a protein-fat, very low GI carb meal), but is just a little lighter. It should be accompanied by carbohydrates with a very low GI (35 or less) and consist of less fat and more fresh vegetables.

Appetizers

Choose or make a salad or soup that only contains carbohydrates with a very low GI (35 or less).

Main course with a high protein content

The best choices are: lean meat, such as chicken or turkey; raw, poached, or steamed fish; eggs (on occasion); and vegetable sides such as steamed leeks, cabbage, broccoli, and cauliflower.

Dessert

Try apple compote without sugar, or cooked fruit (but not bananas). You can also eat raw fruit as long as it does not cause digestive problems. Choose berries such as strawberries, raspberries, and blueberries. At the end of a meal you should forego cheese, since it is too fatty, and replace it with yogurt, quark, curd-style cottage cheese, or cottage cheese.

CARB-PROTEIN DINNER

This dinner follows the format of the carb-protein lunch, which consists of "good" carbohydrates (GI of 50 or less) without saturated fats, (such as those found in meat, sausage, butter, and whole-milk products). Fats eaten at dinner are more easily stored than the same kinds of fats consumed in the first half of the day, especially if they are saturated fatty acids and trans-fatty acids. In addition, sleep and nightly hormone secretions encourage the creation of fat deposits.

This meal contains no saturated fats and very few monounsaturated fats such as olive oil. As at breakfast, it is made up of the following:

• carbohydrates with very low to low GI (50 or less)

• protein (very lean meat, fish, and skim-milk products)

Main course
For the carb-protein dinner entrée, you can choose from among the following delicious and healthy dishes:

• soup made from vegetables with a low GI such as leeks, cabbage, cauliflower, broccoli, beans, lentils, and peas

• whole-grain rice or basmati rice accompanied by a fat-free tomato sauce

• lentils, cooked with onions

• artichokes in a classic olive-oil vinaigrette (see page 144 for a French Vinaigrette recipe) or, even better, in a low-fat sauce made from lemon juice, Dijon mustard, and reduced-fat yogurt

• spaghetti *al dente,* using either whole-grain or white spaghetti. Even white spaghetti made from durum semolina keeps its low GI (40) if it is boiled for only five minutes. This spaghetti can be served with a vegetable or tomato sauce. (To enhance the taste you can mix in few fresh basil leaves, some fresh oregano, and a dash of olive oil.)

- white or red beans in a meat or chicken stock or broth from a bouillon cube with all fat removed

- whole-grain semolina or bulgur wheat with vegetables, cooked in broth made from a bouillon cube, all fat removed

Dessert

The carbohydrate-protein dinner can be finished off with:

- reduced-fat yogurt

- quark

- curd-style low-fat cottage cheese

- apple compote

- cooked fruit (can also be stirred into the reduced-fat yogurt)

- fresh fruit, if it agrees with you, but no ripe bananas

You can eat this kind of carbohydrate meal three to four times a week or even more if you feel like it. Make sure your nutrition is balanced, though, following the 30% protein, 30% fat, and 40% carbohydrate formula.

If your breakfast and dinner consist mainly of carbohydrates and only a bit of protein (milk products, ham and chicken or turkey breast), the emphasis at lunch should be on protein (lean meat, fowl, fish, and good fats). If your lunch is carbohydrate-rich (a large sandwich, for example) you should restore the balance at dinner by eating more protein (especially fish) and a little olive oil.

The best weight-loss results are achieved from a meal consisting of carbohydrates with a GI under 35 and a high-fiber content, animal or vegetable protein without saturated fats, and a little monounsaturated fat (such as in olive oil) or polyunsaturated omega-3 or omega-6 fatty acids (such as in salmon and nuts).

Length Of Phase 1

If you stick to the principles in Phase 1, you should be able to lose five to ten pounds in the first month. If you have reached your goal after the first month, you should stick to Phase 1 for at least three months more so that your body can adjust to the new dietary regime.

What happens after three months:

If you have not reached your desired weight after three months, then you should continue to follow Phase 1 conscientiously. Above all, it is important that you do not now return to the old, bad ways of eating. This is invariably what happens with low-calorie diets because of their unbearable restrictions. If you go back to your old eating patterns, there is a high probability that you will very rapidly regain the pounds you just lost.

Remember that weight loss should not occur too quickly if you want to keep it off. It can also vary from person to person, so don't be too rigid about your expectations, and give yourself the time you need to lose weight safely and permanently.

The fact is that some people lose weight much more rapidly than others. Experience shows that men often lose weight more easily than women, except when they are taking medications that promote weight gain such as beta-blockers, psychiatric drugs, cortisone, and hormones.

In women, other factors might slow down weight loss. Yo-yo dieting in particular—not to mention the relentless pressure to be slim in American society—has done a good job of torturing the female body, thus making it a bit more difficult to adjust to a new weight-loss regimen. This doesn't mean that you won't achieve excellent results. Just relax, give yourself time, and stick with it.

Overview Of Phase 1 Rules

1. EAT THREE MEALS A DAY AT REGULAR TIMES:

- a balanced breakfast
- a large lunch
- a light dinner

2. NEVER SKIP A MEAL, PARTICULARLY LUNCH. Otherwise there is a risk that you will eat too much at the next meal and gain weight.

3. MAKE SURE YOUR MEALS ARE NUTRITIONALLY BALANCED. Over the course of a day, the total energy consumed should be made up of the following:

- 30% protein
- 30% fat
- 40% carbohydrates

4. EAT UNTIL YOU FEEL FULL, without quantity restriction, and without counting calories.

5. THE ONLY FATS RECOMMENDED are omega-3 fatty acids (such as fish fat), omega-6 fatty acids (such as nuts), and monounsaturated fats (such as olive oil) in small amounts. Limit your intake of saturated fats (fatty meat, fatty sausage, butter, whole milk products) as much as possible, and make fish fat and olive oil your preferred choices. Never eat trans fats.

6. BREAKFAST SHOULD CONSIST EXCLUSIVELY of "good" carbohydrates (GI of 50 or less) and no fat, unless it's good fat, such as olive oil.

7. LUNCH SHOULD CONTAIN PROTEIN, FAT, AND CARBOHYDRATES. The fats should be mainly monounsaturated (olive oil) or polyunsaturated and omega-3 fatty acids (found in fish). The carbohydrates should have a very low glycemic index (no higher than 35).

8. DINNER IS SIMILAR TO LUNCH, BUT MUCH LIGHTER. It should contain little fat and consist mainly of carbohydrates:

- if the GI of the carbohydrate is less than or equal to 35, then you can have one of the recommended fats in rule number 5 above, or on rare occasions, a saturated fat (sausage, red meat).

- If the GI of the carbohydrate is between 35 and 50, no saturated fats are allowed.

9. DO NOT DRINK MORE THAN ONE GLASS OF WINE OR CHAMPAGNE, and make a point of drinking it at the end of your meal. Avoid all beverages with high-alcohol content (including hard liquor, aperitifs, and digestifs)— on very special occasions you may have one, but only after eating.

10. AVOID STRONG COFFEE. Even better, get used to drinking decaffeinated coffee.

Remember that the French diet is a perfectly balanced one. It's neither a low-fat nor a low-carb diet. Its just the right-carb and the right-fat diet!

6

Phase 2: Maintenance

Redefining "Normal" Eating

D URING A RADIO PROGRAM on which I was a participant, a listener asked, "Mr. Montignac, thanks to your diet I've lost 26 pounds. This is a huge accomplishment for me and I would like to thank you for it. But I'd like to know if I can eat normally again, now that I've lost weight."
My answer was emphatic: "When you follow the methods in the French Diet, you eat normally. This is why you returned to your normal weight."

After all, doesn't eating normally mean eating whole grains, more beans, more fresh vegetables and fruits, more fish, less fatty meat, drinking less beer, and using less sugar and fewer products made from white flour— just like your grandparents did?

Or does normal eating mean hamburgers on soft white buns, fatty meats and sauces, sugary or fatty mayonnaise, and doughnuts dunked in glucose syrup? Does normal mean drinking a well-known cola drink that contains the equivalent of 20 sugar cubes per quart? Is this today's norm? Then it's no wonder our children are also at risk of being obese and developing type 2 diabetes.

You are what you eat. This is why it follows that a return to bad eating habits means a return to excess weight. A diet that is not understood as a long-term change in daily eating habits is useless. In fact, it can actually have a negative effect because after every diet, your body will try to gain back several more pounds than it has lost.

Phase 2 of the French Diet is all about weight stabilization. The basic principles of the method explained in Phase 1 will be followed in Phase 2, albeit with a bit more flexibility. In Phase 1 certain foods were prohibited. In Phase 2 there are no prohibitions, theoretically, but you do have to maintain tight control over your choices. Now there is a different goal: Avoiding weight gain. As I hope you've discovered, weight loss does not happen by reducing the quantity of food you eat, but, instead, by eating differently—by choosing the right foods. This is why the feared yo-yo effect brought on by low-calorie diets won't occur during the maintenance phase of the French Diet. If you hang on to all the new eating habits you've learned, the chances of keeping the weight off will be excellent. Of course, I'm also hoping this won't feel like a chore if you're enjoying wonderful cuisine à la French Diet.

BLOOD SUGAR AND WEIGHT GAIN

As the previous chapters have shown, the rise in blood sugar after a meal sets off a chain of metabolic reactions in the body. These can lead to an increase in weight when the insulin response is exceptionally high. The total increase in blood sugar is influenced by the effect that various foods in a meal (or snack) have on each other. For example, eating candy causes the blood-sugar level to rise, but eating a fibrous food at the same time helps keep the rise in check.

In Phase 1, during weight loss, the main rule was to choose carbohydrates with the lowest GI, in order to induce the smallest increase of glucose (sugar) concentration in the blood. Only under these conditions is insulin secretion so minimal that fats circulating in the blood at the same time are not stored. It is also under these conditions that fatty deposits can be broken down and burned, which in turn leads to weight loss.

In Phase 2, where the goal is to maintain your new, healthy weight, the challenge is to keep the total amount of blood sugar of any given meal under 50 on the glycemic index. This total is referred to as the "glycemic outcome" (GO). It is the glycemic outcome of a meal that will eventually trigger the process of storing the fats you've just consumed. A dish of potatoes (high GI) will cause the glucose level in your blood to rise appreciably, whereas if you eat low-GI vegetables that are rich in fiber, the glucose level will rise only slightly. Eat the two together and the glucose level in your blood will rise somewhere between the two extremes, depending on how large a serving of the potatoes or the vegetables you have eaten.

If you refer to the diagram below, you will notice that if the glycemic outcome of a meal lies between 65 and 100, there is a strong probability of weight gain. This explains the elevated level of obesity in the US, where the consumption of very high GI foods that contain sugar (70) and extra-refined flour (85), as well as fried potatoes (95) and cornflakes (85) results in a GO lying well within the zone of weight gain.

If the GO of a meal lies between 50 and 65, the level of glycemia (sugar concentration in the blood) is lower than in the previous case but is still high enough to constitute a real risk of causing weight gain. This is probably the situation for people living in northern European countries, where the diet consists mainly of high-GI carbohydrates (potatoes, white flour, and sugar), which are eaten together with various low-GI foods (green vegetables, beans, fruit, etc). Although the GO of this kind of diet is lower than that of the US diet and translates into a lower incidence of obesity as well as less extreme forms obesity, it is worrying nonetheless.

If the GO of meals is not higher than 50, the level of sugar concentration in the blood remains average, i.e., not high enough to produce an insulin response that might lead to gaining weight. This is the case with most French people, whose diet is composed mainly of healthy low-GI foods (green vegetables, lentils, beans, and fruit, etc.) eaten together, with small portions of medium-GI foods such as baguettes (70), boiled potatoes (65), or couscous (65) .

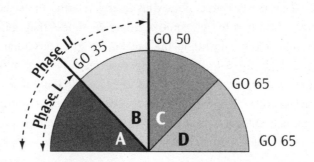

The degree of risk for possible weight-gain or loss according to the glycemic outcome of a meal
A: GO from 0 to 35 ➔ weight loss
B: GO from 35 to 50 ➔ prevention of weight gain
C: GO from 50 to 60 ➔ risk of weight gain
D: GO from 65 to 100 ➔ high risk of weight gain (obesity)

If you want to lose weight, the GO of a meal should remain below 35. This ensures that insulin secretion remains sufficiently low as to inhibit the storing of body fats (lipogenesis), and stimulate the breaking down of stored fat (lipolysis). This is exactly what you did in Phase 1, when you chose to eat carbohydrates with a very low GI and consequently were able to lose weight without counting calories.

THE REAL VALUE OF FOOD

Some people feel so good during Phase 1 that they don't want to stop. In fact, you can follow Phase 1 for the rest of you life if you wanted to, since the recommendations in this phase lead to a well-balanced and nutritious diet. Despite the attractions and successes of Phase 1 you might be ready for a somewhat less restricted diet. This may be especially true if the tight controls you exercised over food choices in the first phase put a damper on your social life. And, if you are a gourmet, I can certainly understand why you might be ready to expand the menu to include a few more culinary pleasures.

One of the dangers of following a low-calorie diet is developing a disturbed relationship with food, where it becomes "the enemy." Too often this leads to bulimia or anorexia, especially in younger people, who are especially vulnerable to social pressures to be thin.

Fortunately, the opposite is the case with the French Diet, which encourages you to love eating all the more! In fact, eating should count among the greatest pleasures of human existence. This is why cooking is a real art—just like music or painting—that is accessible to everyone and which symbolizes some of the most valuable qualities of life. Perfecting this art should not be limited only to an awareness of the nutritional value of food, but should also celebrate the culinary pleasures that come from discovering new foods and different ways of preparing them. For this reason, it would be a shame to deny ourselves a particular food that has a high culinary value, and which delights the palate, simply because it has a negative effect on our metabolism.

This is simply not how French people eat or how they stay slim. What we seek is a balance between two aesthetic points of view that need not conflict: In short, you can maintain a slim figure and still enjoy artfully prepared, delicious gourmet fare in your own kitchen every day.

A TALE OF THREE COUNTRIES

Because of certain circumstances in the past, some people have adopted a relatvely low-GI diet without necessarily being aware of the benefits. For example, in the second half of the 19th century, the consumption of potatoes by poor people, especially farmers, was widespread. Most of them ate potatoes every day of their lives, but did not get fat. There is a simple explanation for this: At that time, potatoes were almost always boiled in water, without being peeled first, resulting in a GI of 65. Compared to the way French fries and scalloped potatoes are prepared today, the boiled, unpeeled potatoes of yesteryear caused a relatively low rise in blood sugar. In addition, the boiled potatoes were usually eaten in a soup containing numerous vegetables that contained a great deal of fiber.

In France, potatoes were prepared mainly with cabbage (GI 15), and in Spain, more frequently with lentils (GI 25). This meant that when people ate potatoes, they were also eating fiber-rich carbohydrates with a very low glycemic index at the same time. The total increase in blood sugar, (the glycemic outcome), was therefore relatively low.

It is also very interesting that the Japanese have not become as fat as so many are in the West, despite the glycemic index of rice, which is above average in Japan. Depending on the type, it varies between GI 50 and GI 70. The reason why they are not getting fat is similar to the one given in the French potato-eating story: The Japanese usually eat rice with high-fiber vegetables whose glycemic index is very low, which accounts for a total glycemic outcome of 50, more or less. These stories clearly illustrate the point of Phase 2: No matter what you eat, you must try to keep the total increase in blood sugar of your meal as low as possible.

TWO WAYS TO MAXIMIZE THE BENEFITS

A satisfying lifestyle is based on good choices, so Phase 2 offers two ways to reach the same goal of putting together an appetizing, satisfying meal that results in a low glycemic outcome (GO). Remember, this means that the rise in your blood-sugar levels after you've eaten a whole meal doesn't exceed an average of 50 on the glycemic index (GI). Remember that the individual foods you eat in a meal and their corresponding GI values average out to the GO, which represents the total glycemic outcome of your meal.

These two options are called "Phase 2 with Exceptions" and "Phase 2 without Exceptions" ("exceptions" being exceptions to the rule of no carbohydrates with a GI over 50). And if you're wondering if there is a particular health reason to choose one or the other, the answer is no. Simply pick the option that comes the closest to the way you prefer to eat under "normal" circumstances.

PHASE 2 WITHOUT EXCEPTIONS

In this first option, you can have a meal that includes:
   • a protein + any fat + carbohydrates with a GI up to 50
Back in Phase 1, you'll remember, carbs were limited to GI 35. Phase 2 offers a widely assorted diet. For example, occasionally, you can eat basmati rice (GI 50), spaghetti *al dente* (GI 45), red beans (GI 40), or even sweet potatoes (GI 50), with meat, as well as drink freshly squeezed orange juice (GI 40).
   You can drink two to three glasses of wine or a beer with your meals and still maintain your new weight. Your average blood-sugar level rises slightly, but it is still low enough to avoid an insulin response that is too high and leads to new weight-gain.

All of the other recommendations in Phase 1 should still be followed, especially the choice of good fats such as olive oil and fish fat instead of saturated fats (which are found mainly in sausage and other meats).

PHASE 2 WITH EXCEPTIONS

The second option in Phase 2 is a little less liberal than the first, but you still have plenty of freedom to eat the foods you enjoy. For example, you can eat carbohydrates with a high GI but only when you balance them out. This means that during the course of your meal, a food with a high GI has to be balanced by a food with a very low GI and a high fiber content. In other words, if you eat a baked potato, this causes a critical rise in blood sugar. To counter this rise, you need to eat a salad or a vegetable with the potato—or, preferably, before you eat it. This will lower the effect of the potato on your blood-sugar level, bringing it down to a GI closer to 50. But be careful! This does not mean it's "safe" to eat two portions of a high-GI food just because you can "compensate." Intead, eat a normal serving consisting, for example, of half a portion of potatoes (high GI) and a salad, as well as fresh vegetables such as broccoli, cabbage, or leeks (very low GI).

THE DANGERS OF BACKSLIDING

Implementing the more liberal eating principles of Phase 2 does not translate into a carte blanche—the freedom to slip back into bad eating habits on a regular basis—on the pretext of simply expanding your options (and your waistline, I might add). It really doesn't make good health sense to return to Phase 1 after you've gained back a few pounds, and then follow it until the pounds have disappeared again. Your body might go along with the yo-yo game once or twice, but it will gradually become less and less receptive until Phase 1 no longer works.

The scenario I just described can happen to you easily enough if you read a quarter of the book and apply only half of the French Diet's principles without understanding the other half. You might even be tempted to view Phase 1 as an easy and unusually effective "diet" that you can stop after you've lost some weight. The trick is that once you've hopped off the diet, it's all too easy to fall into old eating patterns that increase your blood sugar and create an ideal atmosphere for weight gain. You can avoid this mistake if you treat Phase 2 as the core of the French Diet and understand all of its principles. Then you are ready to apply Phase 2 effortlessly, and with great enjoyment, for the rest of your life.

THE ICE CREAM TEST

When I was growing up in France in the fifties, ice cream cones were few and far between. I might have had as few as five or ten a year, between trips to the circus or the cinema. Today, many children have this delicious treat (or similar sweets) which, unfortunately consists of sugar and saturated fats, almost daily. Not surprisingly, the figures you see walking around these days are significantly plumper than they were in my youth.

Half a century ago, a French family like mine ate potatoes perhaps twice a week. Now they are found on the menu every other day. And, in the US, some people eat potatoes a couple of times a day, and usually in the worst GI forms. At fast-food chains, diners, and in many other restaurants—not just the fast-food variety—French fries are ubiquitous: They are served with almost every dish, no matter what it is.

Of course, no one gets hurts by eating an ice cream cone, a plate of French fries, or a sugary pastry every now and then. However, if you do it frequently—every day, or even several times a day—you should not be surprised by the damaging side effects. As Paracelsus, the 16th-century Swiss physician and alchemist, once said, "All substances are poisons; there is none which is not a poison. The right dose differentiates a poison from a remedy." The goal of the French diet is to bring eating habits back into balance and keep them there.

Although Phase 2 is a time of freedom, it's not unqualified freedom. It is still important to stick with core French Diet principles and follow them religiously. But this can be fun, especially when you realize just how much good food you can eat and maintain your slim new physique at the same time.

THE SECRETS OF WEIGHT MANAGEMENT

The beauty of Phase 2 is that there's room to cheat a little—that is, you can eat more high-GI foods than you could in Phase 1, but if you want to keep the weight off, you have to follow three simple rules:

1) If you're going to cheat by eating a particular food, choose the least offensive form. For example, if you really want to eat a potato, eat a boiled potato because the GI (65) isn't as high as a baked potato (GI 95).
2) Plan to cheat ahead of time. This means that you should decide which very low GI food you will eat to compensate for eating a "cheat food" that has a higher GI. The trick is to eat the low GI food first. And remember, you want the total GO (glycemic outcome) of your meal to be smaller than or equal to 50.
3) The portion of the high GI "cheat" food you eat must be smaller than the compensatory low GI food.

REAL WORLD "CHEATING" SCENARIOS

Okay, Phase 1 has worked for you. You've lost the pounds you wanted to lose, and you've been maintaining your new slimmer shape. But now you want to branch out a little and enjoy some of those delicious Phase 2 recipes with a few exceptions that might push up the GI. This is exciting, but you don't want to compromise all your hard work by making a few wrong food choices. Luckily, you don't have to—if you follow the three cheat rules that I explained above. To illustrate, here are a few scenarios that demonstrate how to make "cheating" work for you:

Say you grab a white bread sandwich (approximate GI 70-75) from the corner deli on your way to an appointment. You probably won't find green lentils, chickpeas, or broccoli at the sandwich counter to serve as compensation foods for the high GI of the white bread, but you can probably get your hands on one or two apples. Eat them first, then eat your high GI sandwich. The apples will compensate for it and keep your GO in the range of 50. Planning what you want to eat at every meal is key. That way you can figure out which compensatory foods you want to eat and make sure they're available. This is easy enough to do, especially if you're at a restaurant. Business lunches don't have to derail your weight-management plans.

If you're having dinner with friends, and all you can think about is the strawberry shortcake you'll be having for dessert, don't panic: You can have some. Of course, eating the shortcake is a cheat because it's full of refined white flour and sugar (both carbs have a high GI), and after you eat them your blood sugar would normally rise sharply. In order to make sure this doesn't happen, the rest of your meal has to consist of carbohydrates with very low glycemic indexes. Here's how you can break it down:

- For the appetizer: Choose low glycemic veggies such as tomatoes, cucumbers, eggplant, mushrooms, salad greens, cabbage, sprouts, or lentil salad.

- For the entrée: If your hosts are serving meat or fish, for example, eat it without gravy, sauce, or any other high-GI embellishments.

- Side dishes accompanying the main course: Once again, choose carbohydrates with a low glycemic index such as broccoli, cauliflower, green beans, or lentils.

- You will have to forego bread, even the whole-grain variety.

- If you have a couple of glasses of wine with dinner (and follow the rules above, of course), the glycemic value of your meal will only be medium-high—certainly low enough so that it doesn't lead to too much insulin secretion and weight gain. And you can still have your cake!

But be careful! If you cheat and eat a portion of "bad" carbohydrates during a meal, don't be tempted to balance them out by eating too many compensatory "good" carbs. For example, if you want to eat a serving of French fries, it doesn't make much sense to eat four servings of salad in compensation, since those extra carbohydrates will also be turned into fatty deposits.

WORST CASE SCENARIOS

What do you do when you're at a business dinner or somebody's house and you're served a meal with three "bad" carbohydrates? For example, much to your excitement and alarm, the hostess presents you with a beautiful pâté encased in puff pastry as an appetizer, a rich side dish of creamy potatoes to accompany the main course, and a freshly baked fruit pastry for dessert. In this situation you can easily convince yourself that there is no alternative to simply eating the meal as is.

My own opinion is that this attitude is all wrong since there is no situation in which you cannot exercise a certain amount of flexibility. If you believe in the core methodology of the French Diet, it should be easier for you to resist the temptation of cheating in a really dramatic way. In this scenario, for example, all you have to do is eat the "acceptable" parts and leave the rest on the plate. Gently remove the pâté from the pastry and enjoy eating it, skip the potatoes altogether (and replace them with a green salad, if it's available), and for dessert, eat just the fruit filling in the pasty.

If you're starting to feel that your compensatory measures aren't enough to compensate for your "cheats," you can always go back to Phase 1 for a while.

In any event, the final arbiter of how well you are managing your diet will always be the needle on your bathroom scale. If you put some weight back on again, it may be for two reasons: Either your pancreas has not yet found an acceptable level of tolerance and is still very sensitive to glucose, or the frequency and number of your "cheats" are too high. If this is the case, you should take corrective action immediately, and take refuge in Phase 1 as often as necessary to bring your weight fully under control again.

There is, of course, another indicator of how well you are managing your weight, and that is how healthy and dynamic you feel. If you are unhappy about feeling less than energetic, you will naturally go back to what feels right for you. Options for balancing "cheat foods" with compensating foods are found in the next chapter, Menus and Recipes. If you're careful about your selections, your natural balance will return.

WHAT TO DO ABOUT DIFFICULT WEIGHT LOSS

Some followers of the French Diet will expect very fast weight loss within the first three months. However, if you've been on one diet after another over the last few years, your body has had to deal constantly with reductions in food. This kind of deprivation very often "trains" your body to conserve energy.

If you make a quick switch from a low-calorie diet (in essence a hunger diet) to the French Diet, and eat normal-sized portions, your body can become confused. The switch may actually lead to a little bit of weight gain since your body is still conserving fuel and might take the opportunity, now that you're eating normal portions again, to build reserves (in the form of fat).

In order to prevent this, you should carefully follow the food selection principles of the French Diet and, at the same time, keep portion sizes relatively small. Then, step by step, increase the size until portions are large enough to give you a pleasant sensation of fullness (as opposed to feeling stuffed). It might take several weeks or even months before your metabolism functions normally again, allowing your weight to come down a little at a time.

In some cases, hormonal problems may slow down weight loss. Resistance might also be due to certain medications such as antidepressants, tranquilizers, beta-blockers, cortisone, anti-inflammatory drugs, antibiotics, etc. Ask your doctor to explain how your prescription drugs may be affecting your weight. Taking a smaller dosage or a different drug for the same condition might improve your chances of losing weight a little more quickly.

It is important to persevere and be patient, however, because the weight *will* come off and stay off. The diet has worked for me—I lost 35 pounds twenty years ago and I haven't gained it back—and it will work for you.

Rules for Weight Maintenance in Phase 2—and the Rest of Your Life

1. IF YOU'RE GOING TO CHEAT by eating a high-GI food, choose the least offensive (lower-GI) form.

2. PLAN TO CHEAT AHEAD OF TIME. This means that you should decide which very low-GI food you will eat to compensate for eating a "cheat food" that has a higher GI. The trick is to eat the low-GI food first. And remember, you want the total GO (glycemic outcome) of your meal to be smaller than or equal to 50.

3. THE PORTION OF THE HIGH-GI "CHEAT" FOOD you eat must be smaller than the compensatory low-GI food.

4. CONTINUE TO AVOID EATING BAD FATS (saturated/trans fats). If you have no other choice, try to consume the smallest possible portion, and eat it with high-fiber foods, for example a green salad with vegetables.

5. CONTINUE TO MAKE LUNCH YOUR BIGGEST MEAL of the day, and have a balanced breakfast and a light dinner.

6. NEVER EAT SUGAR—whether raw, powdered, in cubes; or in honey, jam, or candy. Use an artificial sweetener if you find it necessary.

7. YOU CAN EAT BREAD at breakfast—just make sure it's whole-grain bread.

8. AVOID SAUCES AND GRAVIES—most of them contain white flour or sugar.

9. USE OLIVE OIL OR GOOSE FAT instead of butter or margarine.

10. IF YOU ARE DRINKING MILK, it should mainly be skim or low-fat milk.

11. EAT COLD-WATER FATTY FISH like salmon often, for its many benefits.

12. BEWARE OF DESSERTS MADE WITH FLOUR AND SUGAR, especially if you've eaten other carbs during the meal. Stick to berries and dark chocolate (70% cacao). You can also have sorbet and ice cream in moderation.

13. AVOID DRINKING A LOT OF WATER before your meal.

14. AVOID SODA—all soft drinks.

15. AVOID DRINKING DIET SODA on a regular basis, as it maintains sugar addiction.

16. NEVER DRINK ALCOHOLIC BEVERAGES on an empty stomach. You can have one glass of champagne or wine before your main meal, but eat a small amount first—a nibble of hard cheese or a bit of cured ham—so you are not drinking on an empty stomach.

17. WAIT UNTIL YOUR STOMACH is partially full before drinking any additional wine.

18. DO NOT DRINK TOO MUCH WATER if drinking wine. During your meal, drink either water (uncarbonated) or wine (no more than two good-sized glasses a day).

19. AVOID APERITIFS, after-dinner drinks, hard liquor, and mixed drinks, except on very rare special occasions.

20. CONTINUE TO DRINK DECAF or half-decaf/half-regular coffee, and light tea. Once in a while you can have an espresso after a gourmet meal.

Respect your body's pace and work with it and you will achieve all of your weight-loss and maintenance goals. At the same time I hope I have been able to give you a new appreciation of French food and a little taste of how it can not only help you lose weight but enjoy life to the fullest.

7

Menus and Recipes

Menu Ideas For Phase 1

These menus can be served either as lunch or dinner, depending what combination of foods you decide to eat on a given day (the choice is yours). You can either choose the "protein / good fat / very low-GI carbs" meal (the carbs have a maximum GI of 35) or the "low-GI carbs / protein / fat-free" meal (the carbs should fall between 35 to 50 GI). Entries followed by a page number can be found in the recipe section of this book.

NOTE: Use French Vinaigrette (recipe page p. 144) for all salads

PROTEIN-FAT MENUS WITH CARBOHYDRATES, GI MAXIMUM 35

Tomato-Mozzarella Salad p. 150
Veal Schnitzel
Peas
Low-fat Yogurt

Red Cabbage Salad
Mushroom Omelet
Green Salad
Apple compote

Cucumbers
Roast Beef
Green Beans
Low-fat Yogurt

Chicory salad
Chicken Breast with Curry
Mushrooms
Quark

Avocado
Marinated Broiled Salmon p. 168
Spinach
Cheese

Caesar Salad (without croutons)
Basque Chicken p. 128
White Beans
Low-fat Cottage Cheese

Grated Carrots
Pork Chop
Green Lentils
Baked Apple

Cauliflower Salad
Entrêcote Steak
Bordeaux-Style p. 133
Green Beans
Chocolate Mousse p. 178

Celery with Tartar Sauce
Grilled Tuna
Provençal Tomatoes
Low-fat Yogurt

Cucumber Salad
Sausages (Chipolatas)
Lentils
Cheese

Tofu Salad
Bean Soup
Low-fat Yogurt

Greek Salad p. 147
Roast Pork
Brussels Sprouts
Baked Apple

Leeks in Vinaigrette
Leg of Lamb with Rosemary p. 135
Flageolets (kidney or navy beans)
Raspberries

Hard Boiled Eggs
Tomato Casserole
Green Salad
Quark

Onion Soup
Steak Tartar
Green Salad
Baked Apple

Poached Egg on Salad
Marinated Broiled Salmon p. 168
Ratatouille p. 142
Custard

Leeks in a Vinaigrette Sauce p. 142
Fried Eggs
Green Salad
Low-fat Yogurt

Broccoli Salad
Duck Breast with Orange p. 132
Chickpeas with Tomato Sauce
Raspberries

Egg Salad
Chicken Breasts & Tarragon
en Papillote p. 129
Lentils
Apple Compote

Asparagus-Mushroom
Salad p. 145
Grilled Chicken
Cauliflower Puree
Low-fat Yogurt

Tomato-Mozzarella Salad p. 150
Entrêcote Steak
Bordeaux-Style p. 133
Eggplant
Cooked Pears

Asparagus
Turkey Cutlets in Cream Sauce p. 131
Zucchini
Strawberries

Cold Lentil Salad (with Olive Oil)
Salmon Carpaccio
Green Salad
Strawberries

Warm Goat Cheese on Green Salad
Baked Cod with Leeks
& Gouda p. 124
Peas
Cheese

Hummus p. 152
Grilled Sea Bass with
Fennel & Pastis p. 165
Broccoli
Low-fat Yogurt

Vegetable Soup
Brown Rice & Wild Rice
Tomato Sauce p. 173
Low-fat Yogurt

Tomato Soup
Stuffed Turbot p. 170
Basmati Rice
Apple Compote

Grated Carrots with Lemon Juice
Spaghetti al dente
Tomato Sauce p. 173
Low-fat Yogurt

Grapefruit
Lentils with Onions
Low-fat Cottage Cheese

Green Leafy Salad
Whole-Wheat Spaghetti
with Zuccchini p. 171
Sugarless Orange Jello

Baked Tomatoes with Parsley
Asparagus with Lemon Sauce
(Lemon Juice & Low-fat Yogurt)
Low-fat Cottage Cheese

Vegetable Soup
Chicken Breasts & Tarragon en
Papillote p. 129
Steamed Broccoli
Low-fat Yogurt

Cream of Lentil Soup
Whole-Wheat Spaghetti
Mushroom Sauce p. 172
Quark

Leek Soup
Turkey Ham
Basmati Rice
Baked Apple

Menu Ideas For Cheat Foods and Compensation Carbs in Phase 2

Exceptions (cheat foods) are shaded light gray. You can eat these if you compensate for them by balancing your meal with high-fiber, low-GI carbs, marked with a checkmark:✔. Black entries with no checkmarks are neutral foods that have no effect on the glycemic outcome of the meal. Entries followed by a page number can be found in the recipe section of this book.

NOTE: Use French Vinaigrette (recipe page p. 144) for all salads

Lentil Salad ✔
Veal Schnitzel
White Rice
Green Salad ✔
Low-Fat Yogurt

Vegetable Soup (Leek, Cabbage,
Celery, Zucchini)✔
Scrambled Eggs with
Red Peppers p. 112
Green Salad ✔
Cheese
Crème Caramel

Grated Carrots ✔
Broiled or Grilled Cod
Green Beans ✔
Crème brulée

Chicory salad ✔
Broiled or Grilled Sausages
(No-Starch Filler)
Hummus ✔ p. 152
Vanilla Ice Cream

Slice of regular pizza
or White Rice
Green salad with Mushrooms ✔
Apple compote
Low-fat Yogurt

Goose liver with 3 Slices of Toast
Duck Breasts with Orange p. 132
Green Beans ✔
Ratatouille p. 142
Green salad ✔
Cheese

12 Oysters & 2 Slices of
Whole-Grain Rye Bread
Marinated Broiled Salmon p. 168
Green Salad ✔
Chocolate Mousse (minimum
of 70% cacao) p. 178

Smoked Salmon & Green Salad ✔
Leg of Lamb with Rosemary p. 135
Flageolets (kidney or navy beans) ✔
Cheese & 2 Slices of
Multigrain Bread

Cold Spaghetti (al dente) Salad
Broiled or Grilled Pork chops
Green Lentils ✓
Cheese & 2 Slices of
Multigrain Bread

Artichoke Hearts ✓
Spaghetti al dente
Soy Cream✓ Sauce with Curry
Cheesecake

Melon
Green Salad ✓
Chili con Carne
Plum Tart

Leeks in Vinaigrette ✓
Lentils ✓ with bacon
Chocolate eclairs

Split-pea Soup✓
Cooked Ham
Mashed Potatoes
(with Olive Oil)
Strawberries (without Sugar) ✓

Buckwheat pancakes with
ham & eggs
Green salad ✓
Raspberries ✓

Watermelon
Steak
Broccoli ✓
Fresh apricots poached
in fructose/sugar substitute)

Recipe Key

Each recipe includes symbol(s) to indicate:

(V) Appropriate for Vegetarians

❶ ❷ Appropriate for Phases 1 and 2

❷ Appropriate only for Phase 2

Breakfast
EGGS AND GRAINS

Leek Frittata

Serves 4–5
Preparation: 15 minutes
Ⓥ ❶ ❷
Cooking time: 70 minutes

⅓ pound chopped slab bacon
1 tablespoon olive oil, plus more
  for greasing baking dish
3 pounds leeks
1 large onion, peeled
5 eggs

1¼ cups low-fat sour cream
2¾ cups grated (not packed)
  Gouda
salt, freshly ground pepper, and
  nutmeg, to taste

Preheat the oven to 325°F.

Wash the leeks. Cut only the white and light green parts into ½-inch pieces.

Heat a large skillet over medium-low heat. Add the bacon and cook until fat has rendered and bacon is crisp. Remove the bacon with a slotted spoon and reserve. Drain all but about 1 teaspoon of the bacon grease from the skillet. Add the olive oil, leeks, and onions. Cook, covered, stirring often until very soft but not browned, about 10 minutes. Set aside to cool slightly.

In a large bowl, whisk together the eggs and the crème fraîche. Lightly season with salt, pepper, and freshly grated nutmeg. Gently stir in the cheese, the chopped bacon, and the cooled leeks and onions. Mix thoroughly.

Grease a baking dish with the oil and pour in the mixture. Bake until eggs are set, about 40 minutes.

Serve lukewarm as a first course, side dish, or as a main course with a green or mixed salad.

Poached Eggs Provençale

Serves 4
Preparation: 10 minutes
Cooking time: 15 minutes

Ⓥ ❶ ❷

One 15-ounce can tomato puree
4 cloves garlic, crushed
1 tablespoon herbes de Provence
1 tablespoon chopped fresh basil
4 tablespoons olive oil

¼ teaspoon salt
freshly ground pepper to taste
2 tablespoons white-wine
  vinegar
8 fresh eggs

In a nonstick pan, cook the tomato puree, garlic, herbes de Provence, and basil over low heat until warmed through, about 10 minutes. Season with salt and pepper.

Stir constantly with a wooden spoon to prevent splashing. When the coulis is hot, cover and simmer over very low heat.

Fill a low-sided pan with 4 pints of water, together with the wine vinegar and salt, and bring to a boil.

Break the eggs into a ladle and lower them one by one into the water. Immediately reduce the heat and simmer for 3½ minutes. Remove the poached eggs with a slotted spoon and drain on a tea towel. Trim if desired, to improve their appearance.

Add olive oil to the tomato coulis and stir vigorously.

Serve the eggs on hot plates and coat with the tomato coulis.

NOTE: The eggs must be very fresh, otherwise they'll fall apart when ladled into boiling water.

Scrambled Eggs with Red Peppers

Serves 4
Preperation: 15 minutes
Cooking time: 25 minutes

2 red peppers	Salt, freshly ground pepper, and
10 eggs	mild paprika, to taste
1 tablespoon olive oil, plus more	herbes de Provence for garnish
for drizzling	

Slice the red peppers in half lengthways. Remove the membrane and seeds.

Place the pepper halves under a broiler skin side up until slightly charred and bubbled. When cool, peel and then puree the peppers in a food processor.

In a bowl, beat the eggs with the salt, pepper and paprika. Add the red pepper puree and mix well.

Heat the olive oil in a large nonstick skillet over medium-low heat. Add the eggs and cook, stirring continuously, until set.

Dust lightly with the herbes de Provence and finish with a drizzle of olive oil. Serve immediately.

Müsli

(v) ❶ ❷

Serves 1 to 2
Preparation: 10 minutes
Cooking time: none

½ cup whole grain oat flakes
½ cup low-fat yogurt or low-fat
  cottage cheese

1 tablespoon blanched almonds
fresh fruit (peaches, apricots,
  apples) cut into pieces

Mix all ingredients and let stand for a few minutes

NOTE: It is better to eat uncooked oats since their glycemic index can increase in cooking.

Fried Eggs and Cured Ham

❶ ❷

Serves 2
Preparation: 2 minutes
Cooking time: 10 minutes

4 large fresh eggs
4 slices cured ham, thinly sliced
1 tablespoon goose fat (see Note)
  or olive oil
salt and freshly ground pepper,
  to taste

Heat the goose fat or oil in a large nonstick frying pan over medium-low heat, making sure the entire pan is coated. When hot, break the eggs into the pan. Cook sunny side up for 2 minutes over low heat, making sure the eggs do not crisp and brown at the edges. Season with salt and pepper. Arrange the ham slices on individual plates and serve the eggs on top.

NOTE: Goose fat is available is some specialty gourmet shops and can also be ordered from gourmet supply stores online. If you are unable to find it, substitute olive oil.

Whole-Wheat Rolls

Makes 12 rolls
Preparation time: 1 hour
Cooking time: 20 to 25 minutes

2 cups cracked wheat flour
2 cups whole wheat flour
3 tablespoons active dry yeast
½ teaspoon fructose or sugar
  substitute (see Note)

1⅔ cups lukewarm water
1 teaspoon salt
olive oil or sunflower oil

Put the cracked wheat and whole wheat flours into a mixing bowl. Combine, and make a hollow in the flour. Sprinkle the yeast into the hollow, and stir in the fructose, 5 to 7 tablespoons of the lukewarm water, and a bit of flour. Cover the bowl with a cloth and let the dough rise in a warm place for 20 to 30 minutes.

Add the remaining lukewarm water and the salt to the dough. Using a food processor or your hands, knead all the ingredients together until air blisters appear in the dough.

Brush a baking sheet with oil. Lightly flour your hands and form the dough into approximately 2-inch-oval rolls.

Preheat oven to 425°F.

Place the rolls about 2 inches apart on the baking sheet. Put the baking sheet on top of a wide, flat pot or skillet filled with warm water. Loosely cover rolls with plastic wrap, and let rise for another 15 to 20 minutes.

Before baking, cut a slash in each roll with a sharp knife. Fill an ovenproof cup or bowl with water and place in the oven. Bake the rolls in the middle of the oven 20 to 25 minutes until they are golden-brown. Cool on a rack.

NOTE: Granulated fructose is available in many organic health-food stores, but you should only use natural "fruit sugar" fructose, never high-fructose corn syrup. If you cannot find it, you can use sugar substitute.

NOTE: You may top the rolls with poppy seeds, sesame seeds, or sunflower seeds for variety.

Lunch
APPETIZERS

Avocado Pâté with Shrimp

Serves 4
Preparation: 15 minutes

Cooking time: 2 minutes

5 ripe avocados,pitted and peeled
9 ounces shrimp, peeled and
  deveined
2 lemons
1 packet unflavored gelatin
3 tablespoons Sauternes, Riesling,

or Montbazillac
1 teaspoon ground green
  peppercorns
salt and cayenne pepper,
  to taste

Mix the avocado meat with the lemon juice and the ground green peppercorns until smooth.

Heat the wine in a small saucepan over low heat. Sprinkle the gelatin over the warm wine and stir until dissolved. Pour over the avocado mixture, season with salt and cayenne pepper, and mix well.

Pour into a mold and smooth the surface with a rubber spatula. Place it in the refrigerator for at least 6 hours.

Unmold the pâté by dipping the mold into a pan of warm water until the pâté comes away from sides.

Invert the pâté onto a plate lined with lettuce leaves. Garnish the the shrimp and serve with a light mayonnaise dressing.

Endive, Ham, and Cheese Casserole

❶ ❷

Serves 4
Preparation: 10 minutes
Cooking time: 45 minutes

8 endives
8 slices thin cooked ham
½ pound Cheddar cheese with
   50% fat content, grated

Preheat the oven to 400°F.

Blanch the endives in boiling, salted, water for 5 minutes. Drain in a colander.

Wrap each endive in a slice of ham and place in a baking dish large enough to hold them in a single layer. Sprinkle the cheese over the endives. Bake for 20 to 25 minutes until the endives are soft and the cheese is melted and browned.

Flourless Cheese Soufflé

(V) (1) (2)

Serves 4–5
Preparation: 10 minutes
Cooking time: 30–40 minutes

1⅛ cup quark
1⅓ cup shredded Gruyère
4 eggs, separated

salt and freshly ground pepper,
to taste

Combine the quark, the grated Gruyère, and the egg yolks. Add salt and pepper. Whip the egg whites until stiff and fold carefully into the cheese mixture. Pour into a greased soufflé dish, at least 8 inches wide.

Bake at 425°F for 30 to 40 minutes.

Marinated Goat Cheese
with Fresh Fava Beans

Serves 4
Preparation: 20 minutes
Cooking time: 2 minutes

Two 5-ounce packages goat cheese
1 teaspoon herbes de Provence
½ cup olive oil
1 clove garlic, crushed

1 pound fresh fava beans
4 teaspoons balsamic vinegar
salt, freshly ground pepper, and
cayenne, to taste

Cut each of the cheeses into four pieces. Place them in a deep dish and sprinkle with the herbes de Provence.

Mix the olive oil and crushed garlic in a bowl, lightly dusting with cayenne and freshly ground pepper. Pour the marinade over the cheese, cover with plastic wrap, and marinate for a few hours.

Shell the beans. Plunge them into boiling, salted water for 2 minutes and then remove the fine skin covering them.

Place the cheese on serving plates, together with the beans.

Coat with a vinaigrette made from 4 tablespoons of the marinade mixed with the balsamic vinegar, serve.

Poached Oysters on a Bed of Leeks

❶ ❷

Serves 4
Preparation: 20 minutes
Cooking time: 25 minutes

3 shallots, sliced	2 dozen medium oysters
2 tablespoons olive oil	3 tablespoons crème fraîche
¼ cup dry white wine	salt and freshly ground pepper,
3 leeks, white part only	to taste

In a large skillet, heat 1 tablespoon of the oil over medium heat and add the shallots. Cook until browned, about 8 to 10 minutes. Add the white wine and bring to a simmer. Season with salt and pepper. Reduce by a third and put to the side.

Clean the leeks. Cut each leek into 2 or 3 sections and then slice into juliennes about ¼ inch wide. Heat the remaining oil in a skillet over medium-low heat. Cook, covered, stirring occasionally, until very soft, about 10 to 12 minutes. Reserve and keep warm.

Open the oysters (use a sturdy protective glove to avoid injuring yourself and a shucking knife to get the shells open). Detach the meat from the shells and conserve half the liquid, adding it to the wine mixture. Place the skillet over medium heat and poach the oysters for 2 minutes. Remove them with a slotted spoon, reserve and keep warm.

Reduce the cooking juices to a quarter. Turn the heat down and add the crème fraîche. Season with salt and pepper.

Arrange a bed of leeks on each plate and set the oysters on top, coating with the sauce.

Serve immediately.

Sauté of Foie Gras and Parsley Mushrooms

Serves 4
Preparation: 20 minutes

① ②

Cooking time: 20 minutes

1 pound foie gras	3 tablespoons chopped parsley
2 tablespoons olive oil	4 tablespoons sherry vinegar
1⅓ pounds button mushrooms	salt and freshly ground pepper,
5 cloves garlic, crushed	to taste

Clean and slice the mushrooms.

In a large frying pan, heat 1 tablespoon of the oil and sauté the mushrooms until browned, about 8 to 10 minutes. Season with salt and pepper.

When the mushrooms have reduced, drain any excess liquid and replace with 1 tablespoon of the olive oil. Push the mushrooms to one side of the frying pan.

On the other side of the pan, sauté the garlic and parsley over low heat until softened, about 5 minutes. Stir into the mushrooms. Reserve and keep warm.

Cut the foie gras lengthways into 1-inch slices and cook over low heat in a non-stick pan for about 1 minute on each side. Season with salt and pepper. Remove and reserve on very hot plates.

Discard about half of the fat released by the foie gras. Add the sherry vinegar and bring to a simmer, stirring to loosen any browned bits in the pan. Add the mushrooms. Mix well and serve with the foie gras.

NOTE: Ideally this dish should be made with fresh foie gras.

Zucchini and Sweet Pepper Flan

Serves 6
Preperation: 25 minutes
Cooking time: 1 hour 5 minutes

Ⓥ ❶ ❷

2¼ pounds zucchini
4 red peppers
1½ cups fromage frais or
   sour cream
5 eggs
½ cup grated Gruyère cheese

½ cup heavy cream
¼ teaspoon nutmeg
½ teaspoon herbes de Provence
salt and freshly ground pepper,
   to taste
olive oil to taste

Preheat the oven to 250°F. Grease a 9-inch pie pan and set aside.

Cut each zucchini lengthways in three pieces. Steam the zucchini pieces for 20 minutes. Reserve and drain, pressing gently to extract as much liquid as possible.

Cut the sweet peppers in half. Remove the membrane and the seeds. Place peppers, skin side up, under the broiler in the oven until the skin bubbles and is slightly charred. This will make removal of the skin much easier and improve the flavor of the peppers. Peel and cut into large strips.

In a bowl, beat the eggs and then blend with the strained sour cream, nutmeg, herbes de Provence, and heavy cream. Add the salt and pepper.

Spread the vegetables over the bottom of the pie pan, cover with the egg mixture, and sprinkle with the grated Gruyère cheese.

Bake for about 45 minutes at 250°F or until the eggs are set.

Allow to cool completely and then place in the refrigerator for 6 hours.

Cut into slices and dribble fresh olive oil over the top. Serve on a bed of lettuce.

Lunch
ENTRÉES

Baked Cod with Leeks and Gouda

Serves 4
Preparation: 15 minutes
Cooking time: 25 minutes

❶ ❷

4 cod filets, ⅓ pound each,
  seasoned with salt and pepper
2 leeks, sliced into thin rings
2 tablespoons olive oil

2 onions, sliced into thin rings
1 tablespoon curry powder
½ cup crème fraîche
3½ ounces aged Gouda, grated

Heat the oven to 400°F.

Check the fillets for fish bones. Using tweezers, remove any that are still present.

Grease an ovenproof dish with some of the olive oil. Layer the bottom of the dish with the leeks and place the fish fillets on top.

Heat the remaining oil in a frying pan over medium heat. Sauté the onions until they are translucent, add the curry powder and fry briefly (this causes the curry powder to lose some of its bitterness).

Stir in the crème fraîche and spoon the sauce over the fillets.

Sprinkle the grated cheese over the fish fillets. Bake the fish in the oven for about 15 to 20 minutes until golden-brown.

Red Snapper Basque Style

Serves 4
Preparation: 20 minutes
Cooking: 25 minutes

❶ ❷

1 whole red snapper, about
   3–4 pounds
1 bunch parsley
½ lemon, sliced
5 cloves garlic, thinly sliced

¼ cup sherry vinegar
3 tablespoons olive oil
salt and freshly ground pepper,
   to taste
pinch cayenne

Preheat the oven to 375°F.

Stuff the fish with the parsley and 2 or 3 lemon slices. Season with salt, pepper, and cayenne. Place the fish in an oven-safe baking dish large enough to hold it. Brush with about 1 tablespoon of olive oil and place in the oven. Cook for 20 minutes, turning after 10 minutes to cook the other side.

While the fish is roasting, heat 2 tablespoons of olive oil in a small skillet over medium heat. Add the sliced garlic and cook until barely golden. Season with salt, pepper, and cayenne. At the last moment, add the sherry vinegar and bring to a boil.

Fillet the fish. Arrange on warm plates. Squeeze lemon juice over the top and keep in a warm place.

Pour the boiling sauce over the fish and serve at once.

Fish Stew with Shellfish

Serves 5–6
Preparation: 30 minutes
Cooking time: 40 minutes

1 **2**

4½ lbs assorted fish (monkfish, halibut, sea bass, tuna, red snapper, cod)
12 prawns or extra-large shrimp
2 pounds mussels
4 white leeks, cleaned and sliced
1 stick celery, leaves removed, sliced
1 onion, peeled and finely chopped
3 shallots, peeled and finely chopped
3 cloves garlic, finely chopped
1 bouquet garni (see Note)
3 tablespoons crème fraîche
3 tablespoons olive oil
1 teaspoon sea salt, plus more to taste
8 to 10 whole peppercorns
½ teaspoon cayenne

Cut each fish into large chunks and set aside. Clean the mussels in several changes of water. Remove the beards and throw away any broken shells. Then, leaving them in a very large pan of clean water, throw away those that do not rise to the surface or do not close.

In a large stockpot, heat the olive oil over medium-low heat and cook the vegetables gently for 5 minutes, until very soft but not browned. Add 2¾ pints of water, the bouquet garni, salt, peppercorns, and cayenne. Simmer the soup for 15 to 20 minutes uncovered. Add the fish to the simmering soup, first the firmer-flesh fish (monkfish, bass, tuna) and then the flakier, delicate-flesh fish (halibut, snapper, cod) and cook for 2 minutes. Then add the mussels and the prawns or shrimp and leave to cook for 3 to 5 minutes more, until the prawns are pink and the mussels have opened.

With a slotted spoon, remove the fish and shellfish and keep warm in a covered soup tureen. Remove the bouquet garni from the soup. Taste, and adjust the seasoning and add the crème fraîche. Cook for 1 to 2 minutes further and pour the soup over the fish. Serve immediately.

NOTE: A bouquet garni is a bunch of fresh herbs (typically parsley, thyme and bay leaf) that are either tied together or placed in a cheesecloth bag and used to flavor soups, stews and broths.

Trout with Almonds

Serves 4
Preparation: 10 minutes
Cooking time: 15 minutes

❶ ❷

4 whole plump trout, about
    1 to 1½ pounds each
salt, freshly ground pepper, and
    herbes de Provence, to taste
5 tablespoons olive oil

1 scant cup sliced almonds
1 tablespoon sherry vinegar
2 lemons, halved
2 tablespoons freshly chopped
    parsley

Dust the insides of the fish with Herbs de Provence. Season with salt and pepper.

In a large nonstick frying pan, heat 4 tablespoons of the olive oil over very low heat.

Place the trout in the pan and cook for 6 minutes on each side. Reserve and keep warm on a serving dish in a cool oven at 175°F.

In a small skillet or saucepan, add 1 tablespoon of olive oil and fry the almonds over medium heat until golden brown. Season with salt and pepper. Add the sherry vinegar.

Pour the vinegar and almond mixture over the trout, and sprinkle parsley over the top.

Serve with halved lemons for squeezing over the fish.

Basque Chicken

Serves 6
Preparation: 30 minutes
Cooking time: 1 hour

❶ ❷

One 3-pound chicken, cut into
  8 portions
½ cup dry white wine
2 medium onions, finely chopped
2 large red peppers, halved, seeds
  and membranes removed
2 large green peppers, halved,
  seeds and membranes removed

4 medium tomatoes, peeled,
  seeded, and diced (fresh
  or canned whole peeled
  tomatoes)
3 tablespoons olive oil
bouqet garni (see Note on p. 126)
salt and freshly ground pepper,
  to taste

Heat 2 tablespoons of the olive oil in a large Dutch oven or skillet over medium-high heat. Season the chicken and brown on all sides. Add the wine, cover, and simmer for 15 minutes.

Meanwhile, roast the peppers skin-side up under the broiler on a sheet pan, until the skin begins to char. Remove them from the oven and and set aside until cool enough to handle. When cool, peel the pepper halves and cut into strips.

In another skillet, heat the remaining olive oil over medium heat and sauté the onion until softened, about 5 minutes. Add the pepper strips, bouquet garni, and tomatoes, and cook until tomatoes are broken down and mixture is saucy, about 15 minutes, adding a little water if necessary.

Pour the tomato sauce over the chicken, cover, and cook until chicken is tender and falling off the bone, about 20 minutes. Remove the bouquet garni before serving. Season and serve warm.

Chicken Breasts and Tarragon en Papillote

Serves 4
Preparation: 20 minutes
Cooking time: 15 minutes

2 tomatoes
4 boneless chicken breasts
½ bunch fresh tarragon, leaves
  picked, stems discarded
4 tablespoons olive oil
juice of 1 lemon

salt, freshly ground pepper,
  and cayenne, to taste
1 teaspoon Dijon or whole-grain
  mustard

Cut the tomatoes into thick slices. Salt on both sides, then lay out in a single layer to drain on paper towels.

Preheat the oven to 450°F.

Cut one of the chicken breasts into 5 or 6 pieces. Lay the pieces in the center of a 12-inch square (approximately) of aluminum foil. Season the chicken with the salt, pepper, and cayenne to taste. Top the chicken with several tomato slices and ¼ of the tarragon leaves. Drizzle 1 tablespoon of oil over the tomatoes and a squeeze of fresh lemon juice. Season the tomatoes with additional salt and pepper to taste. Bring 2 ends of the foil together and fold down over the chicken. Fold the sides up and over the chicken to create a packet.

Repeat with the remaining chicken breasts. Put the packets on a baking sheet and bake for 15 minutes.

When ready, open the packets, and drain the liquid into a small bowl. Mix the liquid with the mustard. Serve the chicken in the packet on a plate and drizzle the sauce over the top.

Chicken with Apples and Cider Cream

Serves 5
Preparation: 20 minutes

Cooking time: 1 hour 40 minutes

One 3-pound free-range
 chicken
2 teaspoons cinnamon
2 pounds apples, peeled and
 coursely chopped
¾ cup apple cider

1 cube chicken bouillon
¾ cup heavy cream
2 tablespoons goose fat or olive
 oil (see Note on p.113)
salt, freshly ground pepper,
 and cayenne, to taste

Preheat the oven to 425°F.

Brush the chicken with a tablespoon of goose fat. Season with the salt, pepper, and cayenne, and place in a roasting pan. Roast for approximately 1 hour 40 minutes, or until juice runs clear.

Meanwhile, heat goose fat in frying pan, and sauté the chopped apples, stirring regularly, for about 10 minutes until the apples are softened. Season liberally with salt, pepper, and cinnamon. Reserve.

To make the cider cream sauce, boil the cider in a saucepan and reduce by three quarters. Add the chicken bouillon cube and dissolve well. Then add the heavy cream. Bring to a boil and turn off the heat. Correct the seasoning if necessary. After the chicken has roasted for about 1 hour 15 minutes, arrange the apples around the chicken in the roasting pan.

When ready, cut up the chicken, coat with the reheated cream of cider and serve with the cinnamon apples.

Turkey Cutlets
in Cream Sauce

Serves 4
Preparation: 10 minutes
Cooking time: 15 minutes

1 **2**

4 turkey cutlets, pounded thin	1 tablespoon Dijon mustard
½ cup dry white wine	1 tablespoon olive oil
One 4-ounce (or half of an	1 tablespoon fresh chopped
8-ounce) container plain yogurt	parsley

In a frying pan, brown the turkey cutlets over medium heat in olive oil for 8 to 10 minutes, turning once halfway through the cooking time.

Season with salt and pepper. Keep warm on a serving platter.

Mix the mustard with the yogurt.

Add the white wine to the frying pan and stir to release the drippings. Cook briefly, then stir in the mustard yogurt mixture. Heat gently for a few minutes.

Pour the sauce onto the cutlets, garnish with parsley, and serve.

Duck Breasts with Orange

Serves 4
Preparation: 20 minutes
Cooking time: 15 minutes

❶ ❷

4 duck breasts
5 oranges
salt and freshly ground pepper
  to taste

Preheat the broiler and position an oven rack 4 to 5 inches under the broiling element.

Using a very sharp knife, remove the fat from the duck breasts, leaving a thin, barely visible film on the meat.

Dice the fat from one duck breast very finely. Discard the remainder. In a large skillet, melt the diced fat over low heat. Remove any residue with a slotted spoon.

Peel 3 of the oranges and cut into slices. Fry the slices gently for 3 minutes in the duck fat.

In an ovenproof baking dish, arrange the breasts, fatty side up. Season with salt. Zest one of the remaining oranges and sprinkle over the duck. Juice both remaining oranges and add to the baking dish. Spread the cooked orange slices around the duck.

Place the duck under the broiler for 6 minutes.

Transfer the duck to a cutting board and carve into ¼-inch slices. Then, unless the breasts are preferred rare, put them back into the cooking dish and leave in a 200°F oven for 2 or 3 minutes more. Serve immediately.

Entrecôte Steaks Bordeaux-Style

Serves 4
Preparation: 15 minutes
Cooking time: 30 minutes

❶ ❷

5 shallots, chopped
4 tablespoons goose fat (see Note
  on p.113) or olive oil
1 cup red Bordeaux wine
1 sprig thyme
2 bay leaves
½ cup strong meat stock
salt and freshly ground pepper,
  to taste

4-ounce can (or ⅔ cup fresh)
  button mushrooms
1 tablespoon olive oil
Two 16-ounce, 2-inch thick
  entrecote (rib) steaks
1 bunch chopped parsley,
  for garnish

In a casserole heat 2 tablespoons of the goose fat. Fry the shallots lightly for 2 to 3 minutes in the fat. Add ½ cup of the red wine to the shallots and then add the thyme, bay leaves, and stock. Season with salt and pepper. Over high heat, with the lid removed, reduce the liquid by half.

Drain the mushrooms, place in a food processor with 1 tablespoon of olive oil and reduce to a puree. Add this puree to the sauce in the casserole.

In a large frying pan, heat the rest of the goose fat over medium-high heat. Add the steaks and sear on both sides. Season with salt and pepper and cook to taste (rare, medium, or well-done).

Deglaze the frying pan with the remaining red wine. Add the deglazing to the sauce.

Slice the steak and arrange on a warm serving dish. Cover with the bordelaise sauce, garnish with parsley, and serve.

Veal Medallions in Mushroom Sauce

Serves 4
Preparation: 20 minutes
Cooking time: 25 minutes

8 ounces button mushrooms, cleaned and sliced
3 onions, finely sliced
2 tablespoons olive oil
salt and freshly ground pepper, to taste

juice of 1 lemon
4 thick veal medallions (about 6 ounces each) cut into ribbons
1¼ cup heavy cream
nutmeg (freshly grated or powdered) to taste

Heat 1 tablespoon of olive oil in a large nonstick skillet over medium heat. Season with salt and pepper. Add the mushrooms and onions and cook, stirring occasionally, until mushrooms are browned and onions softened. Drain any excess liquid, transfer to a plate, and reserve.

In the same pan, heat 1 tablespoon of olive oil over medium-low heat. Brown the veal medallions, turning them constantly. Season with salt, pepper, and add the lemon juice.

Add the mushroom and onion mixture to the pan. Stir. Add the heavy cream and the nutmeg.

Stir well and cook over very low heat, with the lid off, for 2 or 3 minutes. Taste and adjust the seasoning. Serve.

Leg of Lamb
with Rosemary

Serves 4–5
Preparation: 10 minutes
Cooking time: 45 minutes

1 **2**

4½ pound butterflied leg of lamb
(see Note)
6 pureed cloves of garlic
3 tablespoons olive oil
1 large rosemary sprig, finely
chopped

1 tablespoon coarse salt
1 teaspoon freshly ground pepper
pinch cayenne

Mix together in a bowl the pureed garlic, 2 tablespoons of the olive oil, the rosemary, salt, pepper, and cayenne.

Rub the mixture over the leg of lamb until it is well absorbed.

Place the lamb fat, side up, in an earthenware casserole dish and roast in a 475°F oven for 45 minutes. Baste occasionally with olive oil and the pan juices to keep the meat moist.

NOTE: Ask your butcher to butterfly the leg of lamb for you.

Moussaka

Serves 6
Preparation: 30 minutes + 1 hour
for draining eggplant
Cooking time: 90 minutes

1 **2**

1 medium-sized eggplant
1 large onion, thinly sliced
2¼ pounds ground beef or lamb
¼ cup white wine
2 large skinned and seeded
  tomatoes

3 tablespoons olive oil, plus
  more as needed
¼ cup grated Parmesan
chopped parsley for garnish

Cut the eggplant into thin slices. Sprinkle with salt and drain in a colander for 1 hour.

Fry the onions in a frying pan in 1 tablespoon of the olive oil over medium heat until translucent. Add the ground meat and brown. Flake the ground meat with a fork. Mix in the tomatoes, wine, and parsley. Season with salt and pepper. Cook at a low heat for about 45 minutes.

Preheat the oven to 350° F.

Rinse the eggplant and pat dry. Heat 2 tablespoons of the olive oil in a second frying pan over medium heat. Fry the eggplant slices until they are a gold-brown color on both sides. Grease a baking dish with the olive oil. Place the eggplant and ground meat in the casserole in alternating layers. Sprinkle the grated cheese over the top. Bake in the oven for 45 minutes until hot and cheese is browned.

Garnish with parsley and serve hot.

Pork Chops with Cream of Mustard Sauce

Serves 4
Preparation: 10 minutes
Cooking time: 25 minutes

4 large (8 to 10 ounces each) bone-in pork chops
⅓ cup crème fraîche
3 tablespoons Dijon or whole-grain French mustard
1 tablespoon capers (preferably salted), rinsed
1 tablespoon goose fat (see Note on p. 113) or olive oil

In a bowl, mix the crème fraîche, mustard, and rinsed capers.

Over medium heat, melt the goose fat in a large frying pan and brown the chops for about 7 to 8 minutes on each side. Season with salt and pepper.

Pour the sauce over the chops. Cover the pan and allow simmer for about 10 minutes.

Serve on warm plates.

Montignac Pizza

Serves: 1 to 2
Preparation: 45 minutes
Cooking time: 20 minutes

¾ cup whole-grain wheat flour
1 cup whole-grain rye flour
¾ cup wheat bran
¼ yeast cake (0.6 ounce cake)
⅔ cup lukewarm water
1 egg
1 tablespoon olive oil, more for
  greasing pan

pinch salt
toppings of your choice:
  tomatoes, cheese (Parmesan,
  cheddar, Gruyère, or mozzarella
  see Note), mushrooms,
  cured ham, tuna, smoked
  salmon, olives

Preheat oven to 350°F.

Mix the wheat and rye flours and bran into a mixing bowl. Combine, and make a hollow in the flour. Crumble the yeast into the hollow, and pour in half of the water. Stir together. Cover the bowl with a cloth and let the dough rise in a warm place for 20 minutes.

Add the remaining water, egg, 1 tablespoon of olive oil, and the salt. By hand, or using a heavy-duty mixer, knead the ingredients until the dough is smooth and elastic.

Roll out the dough as thinly as possible, and place on a large lightly greased baking sheet. Bake for about 10 minutes, without letting it get brown. Top the pizza with toppings of your choice, including tomatoes, hard cheese, mushrooms, cured ham, tuna, smoked salmon, and/or olives. Raise the temperature from 400°F to 425°F, and continue baking the pizza for 5 to 10 more minutes until it is fully baked. You can take the cold pizza to work with you and, if desired, heat it up quickly in the microwave.

NOTE: In Phase 1 it is advisable to leave out the cheese or to use just a little bit of well-aged Parmesan or low-fat mozzarella.

Side Dishes & Salads
FOR LUNCH AND DINNER

Artichokes Provençale

Serves 4
Preparation: 15 minutes
Cooking time: 2 hours

8 artichokes
3 onions
3 cloves garlic, crushed
3 tablespoons olive oil

1 sprig thyme
3 bay leaves
salt and freshly ground pepper,
   to taste

Remove the hard outer leaves of the artichokes and cut the remainder down to the heart. Cook for 30 minutes in boiling salted water. Allow to cool and remove the choke from the center of each artichoke with a spoon.

In a large saucepan, heat the olive oil over low heat and fry the onions until softened. Add the garlic and cook until soft, about 5 minutes. Season with salt and pepper.

Add the artichokes, thyme, and bay leaves. Cover with hot water and bring to a boil. Reduce the heat and simmer gently for about 1 hour 30 minutes. Remove artichokes with a slotted spoon and serve.

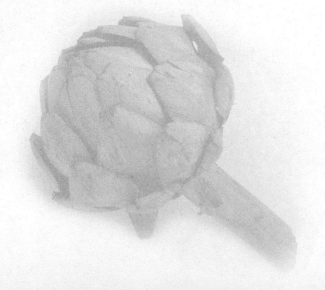

Cauliflower Gratin

Serves 5
Preparation: 15 minutes
Ⓥ ❶ ❷   Cooking time: 30 minutes

1 large head cauliflower   salt and freshly ground pepper,
   (2½ to 3 pounds)   to taste
2⅓ cups grated Gruyère cheese   olive oil for greasing baking dish
1⅔ cups heavy cream

Wash the cauliflower. Cut the florets from the stem and cook for 15 minutes in a large pan of salted, boiling water. Drain well.

In a bowl, mix the grated Gruyère and the double cream. Season generously with pepper.

Grease a large, shallow baking dish with olive oil. Arrange the florets and pour the cream mixture over the top.

Place the dish under broiler for 10 to 12 minutes. Serve very hot.

NOTE: This dish may also be served as a starter or main dish.

Ratatouille

Serves 4
Preparation: 30 minutes
(v) ❶ ❷   Cooking time: 20 minutes

2 tablespoons cold-pressed
  olive oil
10 pearl onions
1¾ cups crushed tomatoes
¼ cup tomato juice
1 medium-sized eggplant, cut
  into pieces
1 medium-sized zucchini, cut
  into pieces
½ green pepper, membranes
  removed, seeded, diced
¼ pound or ten 4-inch green
  beans, cut in two

⅛ pound or ten 4-inch yellow
  waxed beans, cut in two
1 large peeled, crushed garlic
  clove
2 tablespoon basil pesto
1 tablespoon tamari sauce
  (see Note)
1 teaspoon herbes de Provence
½ teaspoon dried thyme
salt and freshly ground pepper,
  to taste

Pour the olive oil into a saucepan and sauté the onions 10 minutes over medium-low heat.

Add the remaining ingredients. Raise the heat to medium high. Cover and cook briskly for 10 to 15 minutes until the vegetables are tender but still "al dente".

NOTE: Tamari is naturally fermented soy sauce that contains no wheat, available in most stores.

Skewered Vegetables Provençale

Serves 4
Preparation: 20 minutes
Ⓥ ❶ ❷
Cooking time: 15 to 20 minutes

8 small firm tomatoes
4 large button mushrooms
2 large onions
2 red peppers

olive oil for brushing
salt, freshly ground pepper, and
herbes de Provence to taste

Cut the tomatoes in half and the onions and mushrooms in quarters.

Cut the peppers in half. Remove the stem and the seeds, then cut into 1-inch squares.

To make a skewer, thread a tomato half, an onion quarter, a pepper, square, a mushroom quarter, tomato half, and so on—completing the row with a tomato half.

Brush with olive oil. Season with salt and pepper. Sprinkle with herbes de Provence.

Arrange the skewers in a large baking sheet and place the sheet under the broiler. Broil, turning the skewer regularly, one turn at a time.

French Vinaigrette

Makes 1 cruet (salad dressing bottle)
Preparation: 10 to 15 minutes
Cooking time: none

1 tablespoon strong mustard.
⅔ cup white wine vinegar
¾ cup sunflower, safflower, or canola oil
¾ cup olive oil
1 teaspoon sea salt

3 grindings pepper
1 clove garlic, crushed
1 teaspoon herbes de Provence
3 pinches mild paprika
1 small pinch cayenne
1 pinch curry powder

Shake the spices, mustard, and vinegar together in a cruet or jar with a lid until well mixed and spices are dissolved. Add the oils and shake well.

Refrigerate until ready to use.

NOTE: Use to dress any of the salads in Phases 1 or 2.

Asparagus-Mushroom Salad

Serves 4
Preparation: 20 minutes
Cooking time: 15 minutes

(V) ❶ ❷

1¼ pounds asparagus	juice of 1 lemon
1¼ pounds button mushrooms	salt and white pepper, to taste
1 small bunch watercress	2 tablespoons olive oil

Wash the asparagus spears and snap off the bottoms.

Boil in salted water in a wide saucepan for about 6 to 8 minutes, until crisp and tender.

Remove the stems from the mushrooms, wash, and dry. Cut the larger mushrooms in half.

In a bowl, combine the mushrooms and the asparagus. Mix together the olive oil, lemon juice, salt, and pepper. Pour over the salad and let marinate for 5 to 10 minutes.

Mix again thoroughly and decorate with small bunches of cress.

Avocado Salad with Peppers

Serves 4
Preparation: 15 minutes
Cooking time: 15 to 20 minutes

2 red peppers
2 ripe avocados
4 small heads of chicory, rinsed
   and dried
few leaves assorted cleaned
   lettuce

2 tablespoons chopped parsley
20 black olives
French Vinaigrette (see p.144)
juice of 1 lemon

Put the red peppers in a preheated oven set at 400°F and bake for 20 minutes until the skins blisters. Cool, then peel off the skin. Remove membranes and seeds. Cut the peppers into thin strips.

Halve the avocados lengthways. Take the pit out. Peel and slice the avocados. Sprinkle with lemon juice to keep them from turning brown. Pit and chop the olives.

Cut the chicory into ¼-inch slices.

To serve, arrange the lettuce, avocado, chicory, and red peppers on individual plates. Pour the vinaigrette on the top and garnish with parsley and chopped olives.

Greek Salad

Serves 4
Preparation time: 15 minutes
Cooking time: none

4 tomatoes
1 cucumber
1 onion (white or red)
2 small green peppers
4 ounces feta cheese
24 black olives
1 tablespoon chopped parsley or
   a few basil leaves

SALAD DRESSING:
2 tablespoons olive oil
2 tablespoons red wine vinegar
salt and freshly ground pepper,
   to taste

Wash and quarter the tomatoes. Peel the cucumber and slice.

Peel the onion and slice into thin rings.

Remove the stem, membrane, and seeds from the green peppers. Cut into bite-sized pieces.

Mix the salad dressing using the olive oil, vinegar, and salt and pepper. Toss the salad ingredients with the sauce. Garnish with the feta cheese, black olives, and chopped parsley or basil, and serve.

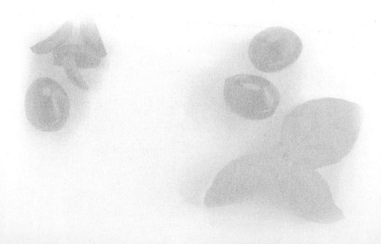

Red Bean Salad

Serves 4
Preparation: 12 hours for presoaking + 20 minutes
Cooking time: 1 hour 30 minutes

1 cup (or ½ of 1-pound bag)
   dried red beans
½ pound button mushrooms
2 red peppers
¼ pound bean sprouts

3 tablespoons chopped basil
3 tablespoons chopped parsley
French Vinaigrette (see p. 144)
1 tablespoon walnut oil

Put the beans in a large pot and cover generously with water. Soak for at least 12 hours. Rinse the beans and return them to the pot. Cover with water, salt the water, and bring to a boil over medium-high heat. Cook until softened, about 1 hour and 15 minutes. Drain and cool.

Clean the button mushrooms. Slice lengthways and sprinkle with lemon juice to prevent them from turning black.

Put the peppers in a preheated 400°F oven (or steamer) for 20 minutes until they blister. Cool, peel, and cut the peppers into narrow slices, discarding the membranes and seeds.

Put the beans, mushrooms, bean sprouts, red pepper, basil, and parsley into a bowl or onto individual plates.

Add a little walnut oil to the vinaigrette, pour over the top, and serve.

Tomato and Green Bean Salad

Serves 4
Preparation: 25 minutes
Cooking time: 8 to 10 minutes

(V) ❶ ❷

¾ pound green beans
2 tablespoons olive oil
2 tablespoons vinegar
2 tablespoons Dijon mustard
¾ pound tomatoes, cut into
    8 pieces

2 bunches curly parsley
¾ cup feta cheese
salt to taste

Wash, clean, and break the green beans into pieces. Boil in salted water for 8 to 10 minutes. Drain and cool.

Make a marinade from the oil, vinegar, and mustard. Gently combine the beans and tomato pieces with the sauce.

For each serving, place some parsley on a plate, place the salad on top, and crumble the feta cheese over the salad. Season with salt.

Tomato-Mozzarella Salad

Serves 2
Preparation: 15 minutes
Cooking time: none

4 ounces fresh mozzarella	1 tablespoon balsamic vinegar
3 large tomatoes	salt and freshly ground
10 fresh basil leaves	pepper, to taste
1 to 2 tablespoons cold-pressed olive oil	

Cut the mozzarella into thin slices. Wash the tomatoes and cut into thin slices. Place on a large plate or platter, alternating a slice of mozzarella with a slice of tomato.

Mix the olive oil, balsamic vinegar, and salt and pepper to make the dressing. Pour it over the tomato and mozzarella slices. Finely chop 5 basil leaves. Sprinkle over the salad. Garnish with the remaining basil leaves.

Watercress and Bacon Salad

Serves 4
Preparation: 15 minutes
Cooking time: 12 minutes

1 **2**

¼ pound bacon, diced
¾ pound watercress, rinsed and
     drained
¼ cup sherry vinegar
1 tablespoon olive oil

Fry the bacon in a nonstick pan over low heat until crisp and the fat has rendered. Remove the bacon with a slotted spoon. Discard the bacon grease.

Return the pan to the heat and add the sherry vinegar. When hot, add the cooked bacon to the dressing, and pour over the watercress. Drizzle the olive oil over the top.

Toss the salad and serve.

Cocktail Snacks & Dips

Hummus

Serves 4
Preparation: 12 hours for presoaking + 20 minutes
Cooking time: 60–90 minutes

1-pound bag chickpeas
One 4-ounce container soy cream
1 onion, peeled and coarsely
   chopped
3 tablespoons olive oil

1 tablespoon chopped fresh
   cilantro
salt and freshly ground pepper,
   to taste

Soak the chickpeas overnight. Drain and put in a large sauce pan. Cover with water and salt generously.
Add the onion. Bring to a simmer and cook until the beans are soft, about 60 to 90 minutes. Drain the chickpeas and place in a blender. Blend while gradually adding the olive oil and soy cream.
Season with salt and pepper and transfer to a bowl.
Sprinkle the chopped cilantro on the top. Serve as a dip with snacks in Phases I and 2 (see bottom of next page).

Cucumber Mousse with Goat Cheese

Preparation: 10 minutes
Cooking time: none

8 ounces fresh goat cheese
1 cucumber
2 tablespoons olive oil
1 tablespoon Dijon mustard

3 tablespoons chopped chives
salt and freshly ground pepper,
   to taste

Peel the cucumber. Slice lengthways into two pieces. Remove the seeds and dice the cucumber.
Drain for 30 minutes.
Puree the cheese, cucumber, olive oil, and mustard in a blender. Fold in the chopped chives and season to taste.
Chill and keep in the refrigerator until required.

Tapenade of Crushed Olives with Capers and Anchovies

Makes approximately 3 cups
Preparation: 10 minutes
Cooking time: none

(V) ②

1¾ cups pitted extra-large
   black olives
Two 2-ounce cans anchovy filets
One 6-ounce can (or ½ cup)
   tuna packed in olive oil
8 ounces capers

1 tablespoon Dijon mustard
¼ cup brandy
¾ cup olive oil
salt, freshly ground pepper, and
   paprika, to taste

Put all the ingredients in a blender and reduce to a paste.
Serve as a dip with snacks in Phases I and 2 (see below).

SNACKS FOR THOSE ON PHASE 1:
Cured sausage, salami, chorizo, rolled ham, rolled smoked
salmon, green and black olives, cheese cubes, raw vegetables/
fruit (carrots, cauliflower, celery, radishes, tomatoes, cherries)

SNACKS FOR THOSE ON PHASE 2:
Canapés made of whole-wheat bread + foie gras, smoked
salmon, caviar; crab sticks, bacon rolled on asparagus tips

Dinner

SOUPS

Andalusian Gazpacho

Serves 5
Preparation: 15 minutes

Cooking time: 40 minutes

1 zucchini	5 tablespoons olive oil
1 large cucumber	juice of 3 lemons
4 ½ pounds tomatoes	salt, freshly ground pepper, and
2 red peppers	cayenne to taste
2 chopped onions	½ cup tomato juice, as needed
5 cloves garlic, crushed	12 leaves fresh basil, julienned

Remove the ends of the zucchini and halve lengthwise. Cook in a steamer until softened (about 12 to 15 minutes) and cool.

Remove the ends of the cucumber and cut lengthways. Remove seeds.

Cover the tomatoes in boiling water for 30 seconds. Pour off water and peel off the split skins. Cut open and remove seeds.

Cut the peppers in half lengthways, remove membrane and seeds, place on a tray, and put under the broiler skin side up until the skin bubbles and chars slightly. Peel.

In a blender, puree half the cucumber, the zucchini, half the peppers, three-quarters of the tomatoes, the onions, garlic, olive oil, and the lemon juice. Add salt, freshly ground pepper, and cayenne and puree again. If the mixture is too thick, thin with tomato juice. Place in the refrigerator for at least 4 hours.

Before serving, cut the rest of the cucumber, tomatoes, and peppers into cubes and serve separately as an accompaniment to the gazpacho. Sprinkle basil over the top.

NOTE: Gazpacho can be served extra cold with the addition of ice cubes.

Smooth Cucumber Soup with Greek Yogurt

Serves 4
Preparation: 20 minutes
Chilling time: 2–5 hours

Ⓥ ❶ ❷

2 cucumbers	salt and freshly ground pepper,
2½ cups Greek yogurt	to taste
juice of two lemons	1 bunch parsley, chopped
5 leaves fresh mint	2 tomatoes
1 tablespoon olive oil	

Peel the cucumber, remove the seeds, and place in a food processor or blender with the yogurt, lemon juice, mint, olive oil, salt, and pepper. Puree.

Transfer the liquid to the refrigerator for at least 2 hours, up to 5 hours.

Pour the boiling water over the tomatoes and leave for 30 seconds. Quarter, then peel the tomatoes and remove the seeds. Dice finely and reserve.

Serve the soup very cold and garnish with the diced tomatoes and freshly chopped parsley.

Chicken-Vegetable Soup

(v) ❶ ❷

Serves 4
Preparation: 40 minutes
Cooking time: 25 minutes

2 pounds leeks, washed and
sliced into rings
4 to 5 stalks celery, washed and
cut into small pieces
1 pound skinless chicken breasts
cut into strips
1 pound tomatoes, skinned,
seeded and cut into 8 pieces

4 cups chicken stock (homemade
preferable, with fat removed,
or organic canned)
1 tablespoon olive oil
salt and freshly ground pepper,
herbes de Provence, to taste
celery leaves as garnish

In a large saucepan, heat the oil over medium-high heat. Add the chicken and sauté until cooked through, about 8 to 10 minutes.

Remove the chicken from the pan and set aside. Add the leeks and celery pieces to the pan and sauté until softened, about 10 minutes. Season with herbes de Provence, salt, and pepper.

Add the chicken stock, cover, and cook for 20 minutes on a low heat.

Then add the chicken and tomato pieces to the soup and warm through gently. Ladle into bowls and garnish with celery leaves.

Cream of Broccoli Soup

Serves 4
Preparation: 25 minutes
Cooking time: 30 minutes

Ⓥ ❶ ❷

¾ pound broccoli, broken
　into florets
1 tablespoon olive oil
1 medium onion, finely chopped
3 cups chicken stock (homemade
　preferable, with fat removed,
　or organic canned)

½ teaspoon dried basil
1 cup half-and-half
salt and freshly ground pepper,
　to taste

In a large saucepan, sauté the chopped onion and broccoli florets in olive oil over medium-high heat, until softened, about 5 minutes.

Add the chicken stock and basil. Bring to a boil.

Loosely cover the pot and cook at a steady boil until the broccoli begins to break down, about 10 minutes.

Using a handheld immersion blender, puree the soup in the saucepan. Add the half-and-half. Heat gently until the soup thickens. Season with salt and pepper.

Cream of Shrimp Soup

Serves 4–5
Preparation: 25 minutes
Cooking time: 30 minutes

⅔ pound medium shrimp
2 onions, chopped
2 celery stalks, diced
3 tablespoons olive oil
1 spring of thyme
1 bay leaf

1 cup white wine
⅔ cup crème fraîche
2 egg yolks
salt and freshly ground pepper,
    to taste

Clean and devein the shrimp.

In a saucepan with a lid, heat the olive oil over medium heat. Add the onions, celery, thyme, and bay leaf. Brown lightly, stirring occasionally for 3 to 4 minutes.

Add the shrimp. Continue cooking for 3 minutes.

Pour in the white wine, cover, and cook for 10 more minutes over low heat.

Remove the thyme and bay leaf. Put the remaining liquid in a blender and puree. Return to the pan adding 3 cups water. Add the salt and pepper.

Cook over low heat for about 5 minutes.

Beat the egg yolks and crème fraîche in a bowl. Pour the soup gradually into the egg-cream mixture, beating continuously.

Serve in warm bowls.

Pistou Soup

2¼ pounds fresh fava beans (or dried fava, white, or cranberry beans that have been soaked overnight)

5 ounces (or 8 ounces frozen, thawed) snow peas, trimmed

2½ cups sliced zucchini

4 very ripe tomatoes

2 large onions, peeled and thinly sliced

4 cloves garlic, crushed

1 tablespoon chopped fresh basil

salt and freshly ground pepper, to taste

1¾ cups grated Parmesan or Emmentaler cheese

FOR THE PISTOU:

4 very ripe tomatoes

4 tablespoons chopped fresh basil

5 cloves garlic

½ cup olive oil

salt and freshly ground pepper, to tase

Cover the tomatoes with boiling water for 30 seconds. Take them out, peel, halve, and remove the seeds. Chop the flesh coarsely. Put the beans, onions, garlic, tomatoes, and basil into a large pan. Cover with water. Sprinkle with salt. Bring to a boil and leave to cook over a low heat for about 45 minutes. Then add the zucchini and snow peas and cook for 15 minutes more.

In the meantime, prepare the pistou, which is a mixture of crushed basil, garlic and olive oil, and sometimes tomato, used as the base for a soup or sauce (similar to pesto). Cover the tomatoes with boiling water, peel, halve, remove the seeds, chop, and allow to drain. Puree the tomatoes, garlic, basil, and olive oil in a blender. Season with salt and pepper.

When the soup is ready, add the pistou. Stir, sprinkle the grated cheese on top, and serve.

Dinner
ENTRÉES

Chicken Salad

Serves 4
Preparation: 20 minutes
Cooking time: 20 minutes

❶ ❷

4 small (4-ounce) boneless
  chicken breasts
2 tablespoons goose fat (see Note
  on p. 113) or olive oil
1 small head lettuce
4 sticks celery, diced

4 hard-boiled eggs
sweet paprika, to taste
24 black olives, pitted
24 green olives, pitted
Salt and freshly ground pepper,
  to taste

Heat the goose fat in a large nonstick skillet over medium-low heat. Add the chicken and cook gently, turning once until cooked through, about 10 minutes per side. Season with salt and pepper. Cool and cut into 1-inch slices.

Take the best leaves of the lettuce and cut into strips.

Slice the hard-boiled eggs and sprinkle with paprika.

Dress the individual plates with lettuce, chicken, celery, eggs, and olives.

Serve with French Vinaigrette (see p.144) or mayonnaise.

Grilled Sea Bass with Fennel and Pastis

Serves 4 to 5
Preparation: 20 minutes
Cooking time: 40 minutes

1 whole sea bass, about 3½ to 4½ pounds	freshly ground pepper and cayenne to taste
½ cup olive oil	juice of 3 freshly squeezed lemons
3 cloves garlic, crushed	2 large bulbs fennel, sliced
1 teaspoon salt	¼ cup pastis (Pernod)

Preheat the broiler. Make a marinade with the olive oil, garlic, salt, pepper, and cayenne. Brush the cavity of the fish with the marinade and fill it completely with fennel slices.

Place some fennel slices on the bottom of a roasting pan large enough to hold the fish, and lay the fish on top. Brush the fish liberally with the marinade. Put the fish under the broiler for 15 to 20 minutes until lightly charred. Turn, brush with the marinade again, and broil for 15 or 20 minutes.

Fillet the fish and transfer it to a serving platter. Remove the fennel stalks from the roasting pan and serve on the side.

Place the roasting pan over medium heat on the stove. When hot, add the pastis. Bring to a simmer and scrape up any bits clinging to the pan. Simmer until the liquid is reduced by half, and pour over the fish.

If desired, the fish may be served with a dressing of olive oil, lemon juice, salt and pepper.

NOTE: This is an ideal recipe for a barbecue. Be careful, however, not to overcook the fish. Before grilling, place the fennel on a large sheet of aluminum foil, place the fish on the bed of fennel, and wrap the foil completely around the fish. Grill for 10 minutes, turning once halfway through cooking time.

Lemon Sole Cretan Style

Serves 4
Preparation: 10 minutes
Cooking time: 10 minutes

❶ ❷

6 boneless fillets lemon sole,
  4 to 6 ounces each
¼ cup olive oil
3 small onions, sliced
juice of 3 lemons, plus more
  as needed

4 bay leaves
2 sprigs thyme
1 teaspoon salt
freshly ground pepper to taste

Prepare a marinade with the olive oil, sliced onions, lemon juice, bay leaf, thyme, salt, and pepper.

Add the fish fillets and marinade for 20 minutes.

Pour the marinade into a large frying pan over medium heat. When the marinade is hot, add the fillets and poach for 5 minutes on each side.

Serve with a drizzle of additional olive oil and lemon juice to taste.

Lobster Martinique

1 **2**

Serves 4
Preparation: 10 minutes
Cooking: 25 minutes

3 pounds tomatoes
4 tablespoons of olive oil
2 lobsters weighing 1 to 1½
  pounds each
12 cloves garlic, crushed

2 tablespoons freshly
  chopped parsley
½ cup rum
salt and freshly ground pepper
  to taste

Blanch the tomatoes in boiling water for 30 seconds. Peel and deseed.

Heat the olive oil in a large, heavy-bottom pot. Add the lobsters and cook for 10 minutes, turning frequently.

Pour the rum into the casserole and flambé.

Add the garlic. Then, after a couple of minutes add the tomatoes and the parsley. Season with salt and pepper.

Reduce the heat, cover, and allow to simmer gently for 15 minutes.

Marinated Broiled Salmon

Serves 4
Preparation: 1 hour marinating + 10 minutes
Cooking time: 10 minutes

❶ ❷

4 salmon fillets (½ pound each)

MARINADE:
½ cup dry white wine
2 tablespoons fresh lemon juice
2 teaspoons cold-pressed
  olive oil

2 large garlic cloves, smashed
½ teaspoon dried thyme
½ teaspoon dried tarragon
salt and freshly ground pepper,
  to taste

Mix the marinade ingredients in a bowl. Add the salmon fillets and coat well with the marinade. Place the bowl in the refrigerator for 1 hour to marinate.

Preheat the broiler in the oven.

Place the salmon fillets in an ovenproof dish and broil for about 5 minutes on each side until lightly browned and fish is just cooked through.

Prawns with Green Peppercorns

Serves 4
Preparation: 25 minutes
Cooking: 20 minutes

❶ ❷

3 shallots, sliced
¾ cup dry white wine
1 pound large prawns, unpeeled
¼ cup crème fraîche

1 tablespoon olive oil
2 tablespoons green peppercorns

In a large pot over low heat, fry the shallots in the olive oil until translucent. Add the white wine and simmer for 2 minutes.

Add the prawns and cook over high heat for 5 minutes.

Remove the prawns and reserve on a serving dish.

Add the peppercorns to the cooking juices and reduce by half. Turn down the heat and add the crème fraîche. Cook for 2 minutes. Reserve and keep warm.

Peel the prawns. Add the tails to the sauce and heat for 2 to 3 minutes before serving.

Stuffed Turbot

Serves 4
Preparation: 30 minutes
Cooking time: 25 minutes

1 **2**

4 turbot fillets
¼ pound fresh shrimp, peeled
2 tablespoons plain yogurt
1 egg white
2 teaspoons finely chopped
   fresh chives
½ teaspoon paprika
1 cup spinach leaves, washed
   and stems removed
¼ cup dry white wine
1 tablespoon fresh lemon juice
salt and pepper to taste

SAUCE:
1 tablespoon olive oil
1 scallion, sliced
¾ cup chicken stock (homemade
   preferable, with fat removed,
   or organic canned)
1 pinch saffron
1 pinch curry powder
1 pinch onion powder
salt and freshly ground pepper,
   to taste
3 tablespoons half-and-half

Heat the oven to 400°F.

Puree the shrimp and yogurt in a blender. Place in a bowl and set aside.

Whip the egg white in another bowl until stiff. Mix in the pureed shrimp, then add the chives and paprika.

Blanch the spinach leaves in boiling water for 30 to 60 seconds. Set aside.

Place 2 of the fish fillets in an ovenproof dish.

Spread the pureed shrimp and the spinach on the fillets. Pour the white wine and lemon juice over the fish. Place the two remaining fish fillets on top. Season with salt and pepper.

Cover the dish with aluminium foil and bake in the oven for 10 to 15 minutes until the fish is done and easily flaked with a fork.

In the meantime, sauté the sliced scallion in a saucepan in the olive oil, over medium heat. Add the chicken stock and the spices. Cook on low heat for 2 minutes. Add the cream. Stirring occasionally, cook on a medium heat for 5 minutes until the sauce is hot. Season with salt and pepper.

Pour the sauce over the fish fillets and serve.

Whole Wheat Spaghetti with Zucchini

Serves 4
Preparation Time: 10 minutes
Cooking time: 10 minutes

(V) ① ②

1 pound whole wheat spaghetti
1 pound zucchini
salt and freshly ground pepper,
 to taste

juice of one lemon
1 cup low-fat sour cream
2 tablespoons Dijon mustard
few leaves basil, chopped

Wash the zucchini and cut into cubes. Steam the zucchini in the lemon juice in a covered nonstick frying pan over medium heat until tender. Season with salt and pepper.

Heat the sour cream, mustard, and basil in a saucepan.

Cook the spaghetti for 12 minutes in salted water. Drain.

Put the spaghetti on a serving plate, arranging the zucchini cubes around the pasta, cover with sauce and serve.

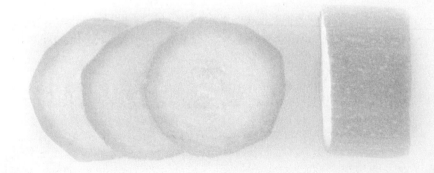

Mushroom Sauce

Makes approximately 3 cups sauce
Preparation: 20 minutes
Cooking time: 10 minutes

½ pound fresh or canned white mushrooms
½ pound fresh porcini or cremini mushrooms
½ cup low-fat yogurt
1 bunch fresh basil, finely chopped, or 1 tablespoon crumbled dried basil

5 to 6 garlic cloves, crushed
1 teaspoon dried tarragon
salt and freshly ground pepper, to taste
1 tablespoon olive oil

Clean or drain the mushrooms.

Slice the porcini thinly. Heat the olive oil in a large frying pan over medium heat and sauté the porcini for a few minutes. In a blender, purée the white mushrooms and half of the cooked porcini, adding some of the yogurt if needed. Add the puree to the skillet with the remaining porcini pieces, along with the basil, garlic, and the remaining yogurt. Season with salt, pepper, and tarragon.

Heat gently over low heat so the sauce doesn't burn.

NOTE: Other than the olive oil, there is no fat in this sauce, so it can be served as a carbohydrate meal with spaghetti. Also, this sauce can also be made without porcini using 1 pound of white mushrooms.

Tomato Sauce

Makes 3 cups sauce
Preparation Time: 10 minutes

ⓥ ❶ ❷

Cooking time: 20 minutes

2 cups or one 15-ounce can
tomato puree
3 large onions
6 garlic cloves
½ cup fresh basil leaves, finely
chopped, or 2 tablespoons
crumbled, dried, basil

2 tablespoons herbes de Provence
⅔ cup low-fat yogurt

Puree the onions and garlic cloves in a blender. If needed, add a bit of water to make the mixture creamier.

Cook the mixture at very low heat in a large nonstick frying pan until raw flavor is gone, about 10 minutes. Add the tomato puree, the garlic-onion puree, the basil, the mixed herbs, and the yogurt.

Cook for 10 minutes over low heat.

NOTE: This recipe contains no fat. You can therefore serve it with whole-wheat spaghetti, spaghetti *al dente,* or brown rice.

Desserts

Apple-Nut Torte

 ②

Serves 4
Preparation Time: 30 minutes
Baking time: 35 minutes

TORTE BASE:
1 cup ground hazelnuts
¾ cup ground almonds
⅓ cup granulated fructose (see Note on p.114) or sugar substitute
3 egg whites

FILLING:
4 apples
juice of half a lemon

¾ cup water
2 tablespoons fructose or sugar substitute
3 tablespoons sugar-free apricot jam
2 tablespoons high-quality margarine

Preheat the oven to 350°F.

For the torte base: Whip the egg whites and fructose or sugar substitute until stiff. Fold in the ground hazelnuts and almonds. Place a heatproof, 8-inch removable-bottom tart pan on baking parchment on a baking sheet. Press the nut mixture into the pan, being sure it reaches all the way up the sides. Bake for 20 minutes or until set.

In the meantime, peel the apples. Cut two of the peeled apples into cubes. Place in a saucepan with the juice of half a lemon and ½ cup water. Cook over medium heat, stirring often, until apples are completely soft and breaking down. Using a fork, mash the apples until smooth, forming a compote.

Remove the tart pan from the oven and let cool for a few minutes.

Cut the remaining 2 apples in half. Carefully remove their cores and cut into thin half-moon slices. Spread the apple compote over the tart. Arrange the apple slices in a rose pattern on top of the apple compote. Sprinkle with fructose or sugar substitute. Cut the margarine into small pieces and distribute over the torte. Return to the oven and bake at 400°F for a further 15 minutes. Remove from the oven and cool. Melt the apricot jam with ¼ cup of water and use to glaze the torte.

NOTE: By adding a pinch of salt to the egg whites (when whipping them), they become even stiffer.

Brazilian Mousse

Serves 6
Preparation: 20 minutes
Cooking time: 10 minutes

4 tablespoons instant coffee
¾ cup whipping cream
¼ cup rum
⅓ heaping cup granulated
   low-GI fructose (see Note on
   p. 114) or sugar substitute

1 envelope gelatin
6 eggs, separated
pinch salt
coarsely ground coffee beans

In a double-boiler set over simmering water, dissolve the instant coffee in the cream and rum. Add the fructose or sugar substitute, and dissolve.

Sprinkle the gelatin over cold water in a small bowl and allow to soften for 5 minutes. Add to the coffee mixture and dissolve. Allow to cool.

In the bowl of an electric mixer, add a pinch of salt to the whites and whisk until very stiff.

Mix the coffee cream with the egg yolks. Fold the whites carefully into the coffee mixture with a spatula.

Transfer to a glass serving bowl, or 6 small individual molds.

Refrigerate for 5 to 6 hours.

Before serving, sprinkle with freshly ground coffee beans.

Chocolate Mousse

Ⓥ ❷

Serves 6–8
Preparation: 25 minutes
Chilling time: at least 6 hours

14 ounces dark chocolate
   (at least 70% cacao content)
4 teaspoons instant coffee
zest of 1 orange (organic preferred)
8 eggs
1 pinch salt

Break the chocolate into pieces and place in a double boiler. Mix the coffee with ½ cup of water and the rum, and add to the chocolate. Melt the chocolate, stirring constantly over a low heat. If the mixture is too solid, add a bit of water. When the chocolate has melted and the mixture is smooth, remove the saucepan from the stove.

Add half of the orange zest to the pot and stir. Separate the eggs into two mixing bowls—the egg whites in one, the egg yolks in another. Whip the egg whites, along with a pinch of salt, until stiff. Add the the chocolate to the egg yolks, stirring until the mixture has a smooth consistency. Gently fold this mixture into the egg whites. Make sure that the egg whites are well incorporated and no chocolate is left at the bottom of the bowl.

You can either leave the mousse in the mixing bowl, first cleaning the rim, or transfer it to a serving bowl or to small individual bowls. Sprinkle the remaining grated orange peel over the mousse and cool in the refrigerator for at least 6 hours.

Chocolate Orange Cognac Cake

Serves 4 to 6
Preparation: 25 minutes
Cooking time: 30 minutes

olive oil for greasing pan
9 ounces bittersweet chocolate (at least 70% cacao content)
1 teaspoon orange zest
5 eggs, separated
¼ cup cold water
2 tablespoons cognac
pinch salt

Preheat the oven to 325°F. Grease an 8-inch cake pan olive oil and set aside.

Put the chocolate in a heat-proof bowl and set over a saucepan with just simmering water. Heat until chocolate is melted and smooth. Remove from the heat and stir half of the zest. Allow to cool.

Once cool, whisk in the egg yolks along with the water and cognac until smooth.

In the bowl of an electric mixer, beat the egg whites with the pinch of salt until firm and glossy. Carefully fold the whites into the chocolate mixture until just incorporated.

Pour the batter into the prepared pan, sprinkle the remaining zest over the top, and bake until just set and a toothpick inserted in the center comes out clean, about 20 minutes.

NOTE: Serve with whipped cream or vanilla ice cream during Phase 2.

Fruit Smoothie

(V) ❶ ❷

Serves 1
Preparation: 5 minutes
Cooking time: none

¾ cup skim milk
2 large strawberries, ¼ cup
   raspberries, and ¼ cup
   blackberries (fresh or frozen)

1 tablespoon low-fat plain yogurt
granulated fructose (see Note on
   p.114) or sugar substitute,
   to taste

Using either a blender or hand-held immersion blender, blend all the ingredients into a milkshake. Serve immediately.

NOTE: If you cannot find one of the berries, use more of one of the others.

Raspberry-Yogurt Ice Cream

Serves 4
Preparation: 15 minutes
Freezing time: at least 8 hours

(V) **1** **2**

1 cup low-fat yogurt
1¼ cups (about half of a pint
  basket) raspberries, fresh or
  frozen
1 large egg white, beaten
  until stiff

In a blender, puree the yogurt and raspberries. Pour the puree into a large ice-cube tray and leave in the freezer for at least 8 hours.

Cut the frozen mixture into small pieces with a knife. Puree again in the blender.

Add the stiffly beaten egg white and mix thoroughly.

Serve immediately.

NOTE: During Phase 2, this dessert can also be prepared using plain yogurt and, eventually, 3 tablespoons of granulated fructose (see Note on p.114) or sugar substitute.

Appendixes

Appendix 1—Measuring Your BMI

People who are concerned about their weight usually try to rate themselves on a standard scale in order to find out how much excess weight they might be carrying. For a long time, there were only relatively arbitrary tables that did not give a precise idea of what a normal weight should be, and what constituted obesity. This made comparisons between different countries or time periods difficult.

Since the beginning of the 1990s, a reliable formula has gradually gained acceptance. This is the known as the Body Mass Index (BMI). Internationally, this formula is considered almost official. It is calculated by dividing a person's weight in pounds by the square of his or her height in inches, and then multiplying that figure by 703:

$$BMI = \frac{Weight\ (in\ pounds)}{Height\ (in\ inches)^2} \times 703$$

For men, a value of 20 to 25 is considered normal; for women, 19 to 24.

Example for a man who weighs 172 pounds and is 71 inches (5'11") tall:

$$BMI = \frac{172\ lb}{71 \times 71\ in} = \frac{172}{5041} \times 703 = 24$$

Example for a woman who weighs 125 pounds and is 65 inches (5'5") tall:

$$BMI = \frac{125\ lb}{65 \times 65\ in} = \frac{125}{4225} \times 703 = 21$$

Assessment criteria for the BMI:

	BMI Men	BMI Women
Normal weight	20–25	19–24
Overweight	26–30	25–29
Obese	31–40	30–39
Very obese	over 40	over 39

A person is considered obese when their proportion of fat is 20% over the average. But how can one determine the exact ratio of fat to body weight in a person? It is likely that a weight lifter has more muscles and less fat than a

Japanese Sumo wrestler who weighs the same amount! The BMI allows you to estimate your amount of body fat relatively well. There is also a way of determining body fat exactly—the Bioelectrical Impedance Analysis (BIA) device, which can be found in some physicians' offices, gyms, health clinics, and schools. When undergoing BIA, you are attached to a machine similar to an electrocardiograph. The amount of water, muscle, and body fat in your body is displayed on a monitor. Using this machine, body fat can be precisely measured and its change during the weight-loss phase observed.

Similar measuring devices, such as electronic scales that analyze body fat, have been on the market for a while. They are acceptable for general use, but not as precise as the professional version.

DISTRIBUTION OF BODY FAT

The real problem is the distribution of fat in the body. To measure this, all you need is a simple measuring tape. Measure your hips at the widest point, and your waist circumference at the height of your navel. The ratio of the two values (waist divided by hip circumference) should normally lie between 0.85 and 1 for men, and between 0.65 and 0.85 for women.

If the ratio is too high, it can indicate android obesity, where the fat collects mainly in the upper half of the body—face, neck, chest, and belly above the navel (sometimes called "beer belly"). This type of obesity leads to metabolic complications such as:

- type 2 diabetes
- increased insulin secretion (hyperinsulism)
- increased cholesterol levels (hypercholesterolemia)
- increased blood fat levels (hypertriglyceremia)
- high blood pressure
- coronary disease

In this kind of obesity, the fat cells (adipocytes) become enlarged by the extra fat. However, their number usually is not larger than average and they are metabolically active. With an appropriate diet such as the French Diet, it is possible to get rid of this fat and to shrink the adipocytes to a normal size.

A high ratio can also indicate gynoid obesity, where fat dominates the lower half of the body—the abdomen below the navel, the hips, the upper thighs, and the buttocks. Cellulite often appears as well. Metabolic illnesses do not frequently occur in gynoid obesity but it frequently leads to poor arteries, and knee and hip arthritis. Women are affected more frequently by this type of obesity, which is often considered an aesthetic problem. The increased number of fat cells can seldom be reduced. Fat stored in this way is much denser and is harder to get rid of. In olden days, it served as an energy reserve for possible pregnancies or lactation, when women often had to face a possible lack of food. Luckily, in most parts of the world today, building fatty deposits in case of times of starvation is no longer relevant, but some people's bodies retain this reflex.

Appendix 2—Exercise

It is interesting that over the last 50 years the number of jogging and fitness-training fans in North America, as well as in Europe, has risen just as much as the prevalence of obesity. But it would not be honest to insinuate a correlation between the two phenomena. However, one must admit that the exercise craze of these last decades has had about as much effect on slowing the obesity epidemic as the increased consumption of fat-free products or sugarless sweeteners.

For many years the whole of America has been convinced that the best way to slim is to expend a lot of energy doing exercise. In 1989, a survey conducted by *French Elle* magazine showed that 66% of French people thought that the best way to lose weight was to engage in some sort of fitness activity. This is a widely held view that is all the more surprising because those who have tried to put it into practice have rarely had any exceptional success. Attempting to lose weight by stirring yourself into action without changing your eating habits is a totally pointless pastime. Though it cannot be denied that exercise uses up some energy, the actual amount of energy expended is far less than you might imagine.

ENDURANCE PAYS OFF

One hour of continuous exercise is much more effective than 30 minutes, three times a week. When you begin intense exercise, your body draws on the glycogen from your muscles for fuel. After 20 minutes, the body uses a combination of the glycogen and stored fats for energy. After 40 minutes, mostly fats are used in order to protect the remaining glycogen. That's when you start to burn up stored fat.

The French Diet can also be adopted for those who exercise in order to avoid hypoglycemia. (Full-time athletes' requirements are more complex and can't be addressed in this book.) With all exercise programs, you should consult your doctor before beginning. In all cases, start out slowly and build up your endurance.

EXERCISE IS HEALTHY FOR YOU

If you don't use it, you'll lose it. Exercise is important to your body's smooth functioning. Taken on gradually and with proper training, exercise can boost your health and mental outlook. It helps postpone aging by strengthening your cardiovascular system and can help to keep the weight off once you have lost it. Muscle gradually replaces fat, which helps you to feel stronger and healthier.

Pretty soon you won't be the one to wait for the elevator; instead you'll take the stairs. You won't drive five minutes to the convenience store; you'll walk. Exercise can also improve glucose tolerance and hyperinsulinism, which can cause hypoglycemia and obesity. Cholesterol and high blood pressure also improve with regular exercise. Mentally, your outlook will brighten and you'll regain a sense of youthfulness. A sense of well-being will return, too. Your metabolism will improve, which will help you to lose and maintain your weight.

KEEP PERSPECTIVE

Too much exercise can become extreme, and in some cases, addictive. Don't overdo it—give your body time to rest. Drink plenty of water before, during, and after exercising to keep yourself well-hydrated. By combining a healthy diet and reasonable physical exercise, you'll reach a level of peace, optimism, and joie de vivre.

Bibliography

CHAPTER 1

BELILLE, F. "Obesity and Food Intake in Children." *Appetite.* (1988): Vol. 11.

BELLUCK, PAM. "Children's Life Expectancy Being Cut Short by Obesity." *The New York Times* (March 17, 2005).

HEINI, ADRIAN F., WEINSIER, ROLAND L. "Divergent Trends in Obesity and Fat Intake Patterns: The American Paradox." *American Journal of Medicine* (1997): Vol. 102, Issue 3, 259–64.

HERBERG, S. "Results of a Pilot Study of the Suvimax Project." *Revue Epidemiology Santé Publique* (1995): Vol. 43.

KEYS, ANCEL B. "Seven Countries: A Multivariate Analysis of Death and Coronary Heart Disease." *Harvard University Press* (January 1, 1980).

OLSHANSKY, S.J., et al. "A Potential Decline in Life Expectancy in the United States in the 21st Century." *New England Journal of Medicine* (March 17, 2005): Vol. 352, 1138–45.

ROLLAND-CACHERA, M.F. "No Correlation between Adiposity and Food Intake." *American Journal of Clinical Nutrition.* 1986.

SPEIZER, FRANK. "The Nurses' Health Study I." Funded by National Institutes of Health (NIH), 1976.

WILLETT, WALTER C. et al: "The Nurses' Health Study II," Funded by National Institutes of Health (NIH) (1989).

CHAPTER 4

CAUPIN, ANNE and ROBERT, HERVE. "Body Mass Index (BMI) Study." Institut National de la Nutrition (1994).

DUMESNIL, JEAN G. et al. "Effect of a low-glycaemic index–low-fat–high protein diet on the atherogenic metabolic risk profile of abdominally obese men." *British Journal of Nutrition* (2001): Vol. 86: 557–68.

CHAPTER 5

KEYS, ANCEL B. "Serum Cholesterol Response to Change in Diet." *Metabolism* (1965): Vol. 14, 776–86.

Index

Acknowledgments

AUTHOR'S ACKNOWLEDGMENTS

Michel Montignac would like to say a special thank you to:
Suzy, my darling (American) wife who graciously gave up parties and weekends during the writing of this book to help me find the appropriate words and expressions to fit the American context; Monica Lalinde, my assistant, whose computer expertise was especially valuable to me—as I am still a beginner in this area; Ernest Hilton, the manager and owner of the Montignac Boutique & Cafe (gourmet food store, cafe, and wine bar at 160 Old Brompton Road, London, UK), who has become an expert on Montignac/French Diet food, and who helped review the recipes and compile the food charts in the book; Barbara Berger, my editor at DK, who spent many late nights and weekends making up for the time difference between France and the US; Jennifer Williams at DK, who also devoted a great deal of her time to co-edit the text; and Bill Barry, Carl Raymond, Therese Burke, Sharon Lucas, Tina Vaughan, and Gregor Hall for their unwavering support of this book.

PUBLISHER'S ACKNOWLEDGMENTS

DK Publishing would like to thank:
Sherry Williams and Tilman Reitzle at Oxygen Design, for their elegant design and good humor; Wesley Martin (www.wesmartinstyling.com) and Barbara Bowman (GourmetSleuth.com), for their culinary expertise; Barbara Hopkinson for her excellent translation, Ellen G. Sherron for indexing the book; John Searcy for proofreading the pages; and Jeremy Canceko for the cover design.